Praise for *The Advantage-Makers*

"WARNING! Reading Steven Feinberg's *The Advantage-Makers* will cause habitually inspired decision making. *The Advantage-Makers* reveals the accomplishments of extraordinary people who could see what others could not. More importantly, Steven Feinberg helps us demystify the secrets of inspirational decision making and makes us all realize we can be inspiring, too."

—Marv Tseu, Chairman of the Board, Plantronics, and CEO, Axesstel, Inc.

"I count myself hard to impress. But I was highly impressed after reading several sections of *The Advantage-Makers*. The material offers a wealth of excellent information and advice, allowing readers to move from research-based evidence to decidedly practical action steps."

—Robert Cialdini, PhD, and author of *Influence: Science and Practice*

"*The Advantage-Makers* not only helps you avoid errors, it helps you see what is possible. You will be better, and look better to your manager, by applying the know-how in this book. Buy the book, have the training and development department buy the book, and then have your boss read it."

—Shelly Begun, VP HR Xilinx

"I've had the advantage of working closely with Dr. Feinberg on a couple of occasions. Whether you as a manager are trying to build a high-performing team of first-level managers or senior executives, you will find his tools and techniques intuitive and effective. You may not be able to hire him to work directly with you or your team, but this book will get you started in the right direction."

—Jim Haar, CIO, BEA Systems

"Steven's new book *The Advantage-Makers* will captivate your mental and intuitive processes. You will experience many 'ahas' and be elated to find within its pages real life help that can put you on the leading edge of organizational and personal thinking. You will receive an arsenal of profound leadership thoughts and an array of actionable ideas that you will continually refer to throughout your life. So sit back, open its pages, and enjoy the engaging wisdom of a cutting edge thinker and doer."

—Bill Fields, President, Packaging Results Inc.

"This is not another leadership book, but a toolkit for dealing with the difficult and real issues. Steven has provided years of knowledge from numerous Advantage-Makers into a leadership playbook. This should be a reference book for all leaders as we direct and align our employees to create momentum. If a leader isn't using the Advantage-Maker dimensions, you will be left behind and must play catch-up."

—Jim Bailey, President/CEO, Accenia

"Feinberg's unique brand of advantage-making analysis links a sophisticated unpacking of organizational behavior to pragmatic, hard-core business results. He gives you a set of powerful frameworks and techniques to focus and amplify your personal performance, and those of the teams around you. He clearly speaks from hands-on experience with executives and real business goals. Smart and insightful ideas, practical and actionable."

—YY Lee, Executive Vice President of Operations, firstRain

"Influence is critical to leadership; as a technical leader without it, the most advanced ideas fall on deaf ears. Use the ideas in this book and you will be influential."

—Raul Camposano, Chief Technology Officer, Synopsys

"Informed thinking forms the basis of meaningful action. Steven Feinberg breaks new ground in helping executives take a fresh look at their challenges and develop appropriate strategies for success."

—Roger C. Parker, author, *Looking Good in Print*

"Steven's idea of shifting your actionable thinking from a linear two-dimensional to a three-dimensional view has been extremely valuable to me. That third dimension has often been hidden, yet it has also been the key to understanding the situation. I have found the ideas in *The Advantage-Makers* not only useful in my role as an executive, but also in my personal life."

—Don Lundgren, former CFO, Frame Technology

THE ADVANTAGE-MAKERS

HOW EXCEPTIONAL LEADERS
WIN BY CREATING OPPORTUNITIES
OTHERS DON'T

STEVEN FEINBERG

Vice President, Publisher: Tim Moore
Acquisitions Editor: Martha Cooley
Editorial Assistant: Pamela Boland
Development Editor: Russ Hall
Associate Editor-in-Chief and Director of Marketing: Amy Neidlinger
Publicist: Amy Fandrei
Marketing Coordinator: Megan Colvin
Cover Designer: Chuti Prasertsith
Managing Editor: Gina Kanouse
Project Editor: Michael Thurston
Copy Editor: Krista Hansing Editorial Services, Inc.
Proofreader: Gayle Johnson
Indexer: Erika Millen
Compositor: codeMantra
Manufacturing Buyer: Dan Uhrig

© 2008 by Pearson Education, Inc.
Publishing as FT Press
Upper Saddle River, New Jersey 07458

FT Press offers excellent discounts on this book when ordered in quantity for bulk purchases or special sales. For more information, please contact U.S. Corporate and Government Sales, 1-800-382-3419, corpsales@pearsontechgroup.com. For sales outside the U.S., please contact International Sales at international@pearsoned.com.

Printed in the United States of America
First Printing July 2007
ISBN 0-13-234778-4

Pearson Education LTD.
Pearson Education Australia PTY, Limited.
Pearson Education Singapore, Pte. Ltd.
Pearson Education North Asia, Ltd.
Pearson Education Canada, Ltd.
Pearson Educatión de Mexico, S.A. de C.V.
Pearson Education—Japan
Pearson Education Malaysia, Pte. Ltd.

Library of Congress Cataloging-in-Publication Data
Feinberg, Steven, 1950-
  The advantage makers : how exceptional leaders win by creating opportunities others don't / Steven Feinberg.
      p. cm.
  ISBN 0-13-234778-4 (hardback : alk. paper) 1. Leadership. 2. Executive ability.
3. Creative ability in business. I. Title.
  HD57.7.F444 2007
  658.4'092—dc22
                                2007005375

Dedication

To the prime Advantage-Makers in my life:

Terri Jeanne Feinberg, still the one I love,
my wife and partner in life

Samantha Jeanne Feinberg and Zachary James Feinberg,
my children, who refine and test my advantage-making skills
like no other members of the human race could

Sam Feinberg, my Dad, the Advantage-Maker
Jean Feinberg, my Mom, the real influence behind the
Advantage-Maker
Who are both smiling upon me from a great
commanding vantage point

Alan Feinberg, my brother—never bet against him

Contents

ABOUT THE AUTHOR

Steven Feinberg, PhD uses a rare combination of behavioral science know-how and street smarts to provide advantage-making solutions for forward-thinking leaders. He strives to turn everything to the best possible advantage in the face of constraints leaders encounter. His clients consistently say, "I wish I had used you sooner."

Steven honed the Code of the Advantage-Maker over 30 years of studying human behavior and applying his insights to performance efficacy and influence. Advantage-making is the single most relevant skill set an executive can have to achieve personal and business enterprise success. For the past 23 years, he has advised senior executives on key leadership, team, and organizational issues. His strategic shifting approach leads to profitable courses of action. This approach enables leaders to see opportunities that others don't even know to look for, and it creates advantages where none existed before. Clients say he makes smart leaders smarter.

Steven's Advantage-Maker leadership programs have turned around ailing organizations, teams, and leaders. For example:

- Working with a company that was losing customers on a daily basis, he designed a customer acquisition, retention, and growth program that generated a $4 million revenue boost.
- He helped transform a senior executive from an about-to-be-fired legal liability into a much-sought-after leader.
- In the midst of a major economic downturn, combined with a corporate reduction in workforce, a hiring freeze, and implementation of a major global

Enterprise Resource Planning system, Steven enabled a nonadaptive organization to increase its adaptability and save $1.5 million, doing more with less in shorter periods of time.

Currently, Steven is president of Steven Feinberg, Inc. His earlier programs, the Ingenuity Lab and the Leadership Influence Lab, both geared toward rapid adaptation, doing more with less, and persuasion, are incorporated into the Advantage-Makers.

Steven graduated *magna cum laude* from the State University of New York at Buffalo and then earned an MSW from Tulane University and a PhD from the Professional School of Psychology, San Francisco.

For more than 23 years, Steven has taught courses on leadership and organizational effectiveness at the University of San Francisco's Department of Organizational Behavior and Leadership. Executives request his keynote speech, *Snatching Victory from the Laws of Defeat*, addressed in Chapter 3.

Steven's client list ranges from Fortune 500 businesses to start-ups and includes such well-known companies as Wells Fargo, Visa, Citibank, Sun Microsystems, Plantronics, Pac Bell, Synopsys, NVidia, Seagate EMS, FedEx, HBO & Co., Xilinx, BEA Systems, Symantec, Cadence Design Systems, Affymax, Wawona Frozen Foods, firstRain, and Synectics, along with many others. For him, "getting leadership right" means acting as an Advantage-Maker.

FOREWORD

I have been through the plethora of books, seminars, proselytizing, and baloney about leadership theory. Why do I subject myself to this? Because a small percentage of this stuff actually has value. Leadership skills are so crucial, that it really is worth wading through all the muck and mire to find an occasional gem.

The problem with most is that leadership is treated as if it's a formula.

Do this and you'll be a great leader. This leadership technique works for everybody. That's the baloney part!

This may make a leader's job easier, having a formula for leadership and applying that same formula every time. The problem is, it works a very small amount of the time. Leadership is an art. Great leaders are able to analyze situations and spontaneously take leadership action specific to the situation. That's not easy, but it works.

The Advantage-Makers by Steven Feinberg makes it less difficult, and will enable you to be a leadership artist.

Many people think that leadership comes only through experience. Experience is important, no doubt. But all the experience in the world alone will not make you a leader. When you start practicing Feinberg's *The Advantage-Makers* teachings, your leadership experience (or better put, your productive leadership experience) begins. Nothing will make you a proven leader overnight, but the sooner your productive experience begins, the sooner you will succeed.

The Advantage-Makers teaches you how to effectively use the tools you already have—your time, your interactions, your perceptions—the very structure of your leadership behavior. In short, with your existing leadership tools, Feinberg teaches you how to be a leadership craftsman.

The Advantage-Makers provides what Feinberg refers to as "T.I.P.S." (time, interactions, perceptions, structures) to see opportunities, create advantages, and influence outcomes. You will start seeing solutions that, till now, you didn't realize existed.

As Feinberg so astutely puts it, "Advantage-Makers' skill and advantage-making are designed to consistently create superior outcomes in the face of constraints. Resources are leveraged in simple, timely solutions that may not have been initially obvious. If you are not an Advantage-Maker, it is very likely that you will be outmaneuvered by someone who is."

The initial chapter of *The Advantage-Makers*, "How to Shift the Odds in Your Favor in the Best of Times and the Worst of Times," is the essence of Feinberg's *The Advantage-Makers*. Favorable odds are sometimes accomplished by taking the right calculated risks. *The Advantage-Makers* will help you get the best bang for your risk-taking buck.

In the words of "The Great One," Wayne Gretzky, "You miss 100% of the shots you don't take." *The Advantage-Makers* gives you a shot very much worth taking.

—Barry X Lynn
Chairman, 3Tera Corporation
former CIO, Wells Fargo and Company
President, Wells Fargo Technology Services, Inc.
March 12, 2007

PREFACE

If you are not an Advantage-Maker, the odds are that you will lose to a leader who is.

—Steven Feinberg, PhD

Do you know how to shift the odds in your favor?

Bookies—not the type who read books—were part of my upbringing.

Entrepreneurs—people who knew how to make business happen—filled my everyday experience.

Leaders—with their challenges, setbacks, and successes—shaped my professional and business focus.

Although I didn't realize it at the time, I was initiated into a unique view of the world that not many people see—the world of Advantage-Makers. I've spent a good part of my professional career discovering how people like my Dad were able to shift the odds in their favor. This book is an invitation for you to view that world of "movers and shakers" and, more important, to see the levers they employ so that you too can use them for your own benefit.

How do you win when the odds are against you? How do you shift the odds ethically and legally to succeed instead of fail? How do you make things even better when things are already working for you? The answer to all three questions is the same: Do what Advantage-Makers do.

Revealing the Magic Bullet

I'm often asked by CEOs, leaders, and managers, "If you could concentrate on one area—a magic bullet—that is central to success in business, what would that be?" It's not strengthening weaknesses or determination, although those are usually touted and won't hurt. After decades of practical application, I'm convinced the answer can be found in a specific set of advantage-making skills—the most relevant skill set an executive can focus on for personal and business success. These specific skills accentuate and amplify existing talents to shift the odds in your favor. The team with the most Advantage-Makers almost always wins. This book describes the tools needed to increase advantage-making capability to solve the most immediate and strategic problems.

Not Another Leadership Personality Book

The Advantage-Makers is not another leadership personality book, nor is it another off-the-shelf, one-size-fits-all approach to leadership. It provides a set of pragmatic tools leaders can use to see opportunities others don't even know exist. Many books tell a leader to change what he or she is doing if it isn't working, but they don't explicitly state how. The Advantage-Maker approach shows you how, providing you with control you might never have possessed.

There is something different about how Advantage-Makers approach problems. They initiate action and thought, originating new ways of doing things. How Advantage-Makers do this has never been adequately described. This book provides the necessary description.

Influences

I am very fortunate to have been educated by great minds, some of whom you will meet in the chapters ahead, who shared their thoughts through dialogue, seminars, and writings. I noticed that each possessed something in common, though they had different backgrounds and different spheres of influence—each had a commanding vantage point that made it possible to see ways to succeed that had been overlooked.

The ideas are based on more than 23 years of experience in providing advice to leaders and managers, along with supportive evidence from applied research in the fields of social psychology, cognitive psychology, and behavioral economics from the past 50 years. This book is intended to be thoughtful and provocative, not in the sense of confrontation, but in ways that equip you with levers of opportunity.

Method

Strategic shifting is the method used to model the behavior of Advantage-Makers. Underlying the methodology is applied behavioral patterning and positioning. It is based upon analyzing behaviors in everyday interactions—among people, groups, organizations, and companies. The model highlights the Code of the Advantage-Maker. It reveals the four levers Advantage-Makers use. You will discover what keeps sticky situations sticky and how to create unexpected gains in the midst of constraints.

Strategic shifting is not another version of "thinking outside the box," but a way of seeing more clearly what is inside *and* outside the box, enabling penetration to what is important. You shift the odds in your favor by identifying powerful vantage points from which to look at problems, reveal opportunities, and create profitable courses of action.

Pointing Out Pitfalls

Although leaders should be wise, they are, at times, otherwise. This book goes beyond studies about failure and lays bare, in simple terms, the surprising mistakes and specific Laws of Defeat that cause leaders to stumble, undermining even the best Advantage-Makers' inclinations.

Cultivating Uncommon Good Judgment

The predictable "common sense" that colleagues and consultants provide as advice often sets up executives for unintended consequences. Be wary of someone whose *only* tool is a hammer; to them, every problem starts to look like a nail. They bring you their hammer and encourage you to hammer away. This limits you, and worse, the more you use the hammer, the more likely you will be hammering opportunities closed, working against yourself.

Many executives I've worked with cultivated uncommon good judgment, able to see what they couldn't before, and what others still don't. The Advantage-Makers' approach shifts the way you think, enabling you to take a profitable course of action. Using the tools in this book, you can spot hidden opportunities, influence outcomes, and create advantages.

In This Book

Part 1 Strategic Shifting: How to See What Others Miss

Chapter 1 How to Shift the Odds in Your Favor in the Best of Times and the Worst of Times

Advantage-Makers turn everything into the best possible advantage by seeing possibilities others don't see. This chapter describes strategic shifting and finding commanding vantage points to see what others miss.

Chapter 2 Breaking the Secret Code of the Great Advantage-Makers

The set of operating principles unique to Advantage-Makers. This chapter reveals their underlying time orientation, their perceptions and mindsets, the way they interact with people and challenges, and how they structure their work to spot opportunities, create advantages, and influence outcomes. Discover your own advantage-making abilities with the Advantage-Maker assessment instrument.

Chapter 3 Wise or Otherwise: Are You Following Any of the Hidden Laws of Defeat?

Even smart leaders fall prey to pitfalls that prevent them from creating advantages. Instead, they may inadvertently produce disadvantage and have to play catch-up. Knowing what to avoid can be as important as picking the right target in the first place. The emphasis is on how you can steer your organization around the traps.

Chapter 4 Shifting to a Commanding (Ad)Vantage Point

This chapter focuses on strategic shifting to a commanding vantage point and how that leads to a profitable course of action. Most executives are strategists, but not everyone shifts their responses to a favorable perspective.

Part 2 The Advantage Points: The Levers of Advantage-Making

Chapter 5 Adaptive Stretching: It's Not the Best Who Wins—It's Who's the Most Adaptive

The first advantage point: *Adapt rapidly. The person with the widest ranges of responses wins*. Non-adaptive responses are costly. Flexibility and agility rather than rigidity lead to control. Without this skill, executives will encounter obstacles that will constrain their success. The chapter illustrates how to spot unexpected opportunity and use anomalies. Practice the advantage-making exercises to help you adaptively stretch.

Chapter 6 The Game Changer: If You Are In a Hole, Stop Digging and Change the Game

The second advantage point: *Game Changer. Do something that shifts the game*. Counterproductive behavior results from persisting in a course of action that actually doesn't work, but thinking that it should or it will. This pattern of mishandling difficulties turns into recurrent problems. Case examples instruct you on an unexpected method that enables you to doing more with less, instead of making sticky problems stickier. The failed attempted solutions provide clues for creating superior outcomes.

Chapter 7 Move or Lose: Manage Momentum to Advance Your Organization

The third advantage point: *Move or lose. Spotting the invisible forces at play that drive forward movement*. Structure shapes behavior. Case examples show how best efforts are neutralized and why 60% of change programs fail. This chapter provides a set of practical advantage-making steps to position you for forward movement and create momentum.

Chapter 8 Strategic Influence: How to Get People to Say Yes in the Right Way to the Right Things

The fourth advantage point: *Strategic Influence: The Multiplier Effect. Small influential moves, big leverage gains.* Whenever someone makes a request, they are involving you in an influence transaction. The chapter covers four scientifically verified influence factors. It identifies how effective leaders inadvertently bungle, overlook, and lose opportunities, as well as specific practical ways to find unexpected opportunities to put to work immediately.

Chapter 9 Influence Perception: Helping People See What They Need to See

Complete the web of influence with four of the most powerful persuasion factors that are in plain sight to Advantage-Makers, but invisible to others because they don't know how to look. Assess your Web of Influence and expand your impact.

Chapter 10 Being an Advantage-Maker: How to Play in a Different League

Time to apply. If you are not continually creating advantages, then customers, employees, and stockholders will look elsewhere. Advantage-making is a high-level craft that improves with practice. As an Advantage-Maker, you will be operating in a different league.

Nothing is worse than discovering a solution was right around the corner and you didn't turn it.

—Steven Feinberg, PhD

ACKNOWLEDGMENTS

A nightmare—that's what I expected when encountering the editors of my book. An unexpected and delightful surprise is what I found in working with acquisitions editor Martha Cooley and development editor Russ Hall. Both are Advantage-Makers in their own right.

Marketing genius (a term to be used rarely) George Silverman took my ideas and placed them front and center.

Michael Ebeling, my agent, believed in my project instantly and guided me through the bumpy stretches.

A. J. Sobczak shaped the manuscript prior to proposal; Charlie Doris refined the initial drafts; Laura Lee's editing brought emotion into my stories; and Krista Hansing put the final editorial touches on the book. Michael Thurston, the master of book production, made it work. The readers are much happier because of all of you.

All the executives and managers involved—too numerous to mention individually here, but whom you will find throughout the book—willingly opened themselves to interviews and collaboration to create opportunities. They kept kidding me about being in the book. I guess they were right.

Bill Fields, Marv Tseu, Jim Bailey, and Don Lundgren continuously encouraged my talents, employed my ideas in numerous business ventures, provided examples, and emboldened my contribution.

Barry X Lynn wrote the Foreword and shared his talents as an Advantage-Maker.

Dick Fisch, John Weakland, and Karen Schlanger began an article with me many moons ago that informed the Game Changer work here. Karen and I worked together on a project described in the book and completed the article.

Jeff Arnold and Mike Scott helped in numerous consulting and writing projects; you'll find their insights in the pages ahead. Frank Lucatelli collaborated on structural behavior patterns.

Robert Cialdini, the world's leading authority on influence, generously provided guidance and acknowledgment of applying influence principles with leaders. Robert Fritz's work provided foundational insight into the natural structures we live by and work in. The founders and trainers in the field of NLP made the relationship between structure and perception non-arguable and transformed my world.

Don MacMillan, a coach to the coach, an Advantage-Maker before there was such a thing, helped me see business opportunities and successfully supported my early efforts in working with leaders.

Our friends in Palo Alto delighted me with their energy and wanted to have a book signing just so they could get together and talk—what a fun, spirited, and intelligent group.

The Feinberg, Lillianfeld, DeVries, and Chamberlain families share with me the advantage of strong family bonds.

My parents, Sam and Jean Feinberg, whom you will meet in the book, taught me more and helped me more than they even realized. Without their advantage-making prowess and encouragement, I would not see what is possible in the world.

My children, Samantha and Zachary, enrich my life with their own. What could be better?

My wife, Terri, encouraged and shaped my writing— not just with goodwill, but with endless hours of editing, discussing, and calming. She shifts to commanding vantage points to guide our life. Without her, this book would not exist.

PART 1

Strategic Shifting: How to See What Others Miss

CHAPTER 1

How to Shift the Odds in Your Favor in the Best of Times and the Worst of Times

You miss 100% of the shots you never take.
—Wayne Gretsky

Hundreds of years ago, in medieval Austria, a small but determined army was trying desperately to hold on to its fortress against tremendous odds. For more than six months, the defenders had been surrounded by a hostile army. With no way to contact outside help to replenish their stocks, supplies had dwindled to a desperate level. Only one cow and two bags of grain were left.

     The fortress soldiers, wracked with fatigue and hunger, turned to their commander for guidance.

     Expecting their leader to say the expected, "Ration the food for as long as we can hold out," they were astonished and perturbed when they received a different, radical reply.

     "Kill the cow, stuff it with all the grain we have, and toss it over the walls when the next wave of attacks ensues."

     This seemed illogical, foolhardy, and dangerous. During the next attack, they followed the unexpected order and heaved the grain-stuffed cow over the wall. Without a doubt, they anticipated a slow, anguished death by starvation. To this day we don't know why the soldiers complied.

     But the commander had foreseen something that no one else had.

     Confused by the bovine assault, several of the attackers took the cow back to their officer's tent. The attacking officer saw it for what it was—a signal of defiance from the fortress commander, as well as a message that his soldiers had the will to fight on. If they could afford to throw a cow stuffed with excess grain over the wall, he reasoned, they must have vast stores of supplies, enough to last the entire winter. He ordered an immediate retreat.[1]

Uncommon Good Sense:
Doing the Strategic Math

How, you might ask, does medieval cow tossing relate to twenty-first-century business? Although the average corporate suite or management office might bear little resemblance to a stone fortress under siege, the strategy of shifting focus to produce novel solutions is directly applicable to business leadership and advantage-making.

Was the fortress commander a fool who just got lucky? Was the attacking army officer incompetent? Was this just a one-time tactical maneuver, or can it illustrate a dimension of action that is overlooked?

If we faced the same situation as our Austrian commander, convention and common sense would have compelled most of us to use a strategy of persistence. Reasonably, we would have rationed the supplies to maintain our position as long as we could. That thought process, however, would do little to actually remove us from the situation or to improve it. After a week or two had passed, we would slowly succumb to hunger and thirst, and we would still be stuck in the fortress.

The shift from "ration the food" to "throw the food at the enemy" was exceptional. It didn't conform to the general rule or pattern.

The commander did what might be called the "strategic math" on the situation. He projected the consequences of rationing the food. In two weeks, they would still be under siege, but now without food—no better off, and facing an even worse crisis.

Shifting his vantage point 180°, he realized that instead of helping, rationing the food would only prolong the inevitable.

Proceeding along this line of thought, he considered how the lack of food could move from a problem for the defenders to a problem for the attackers. Food was no longer a resource for satisfying hunger; instead, it could be used to send a message. It became a persuasion weapon, the resource to change the dynamics of the situation. Although the fortress commander was driven by desperation, he sent a counterintuitive, resoundingly clear message: "We have plenty of supplies; prepare for a long battle."

This example clearly demonstrates a leader down to his last few resources who outmaneuvers his superior opponent. Military metaphors have their uses and limits for business; what matters here is the illustration of strategic shifting to create advantages.

Most managers are of sound mind, but their behavior sometimes falls prey to a definition of insanity: "If you keep doing what you've always done and expect a different result." Although it sounds comically simple, it is surprising how rarely people follow this principle: *If what you are doing is not working, do something different.*

It is easy to say, "Do something different," yet few people know how this actually works—and fewer still know how to actually do something substantively different. Today's right answer can produce tomorrow's failure. As the landscape changes, leaders must adapt beyond their own plan for success. In the current demanding environments in which leaders must do more with less, they would be well advised to expand their dimensions of action. This book illustrates how exceptional leaders develop profitable courses of action in the face of constraints—and how you can, too.

The fortress commander stepped outside the logic of the battle and delivered an unexpected message. Clearly, he was able to see opportunities, solutions, and strategies others didn't even know existed.

Whether your battle is finding new business opportunities, handling people issues, or creating solutions to problems, it is crucial to step outside the logic of that battle and consistently create superior outcomes.

The fortress commander's competition didn't know he was up against an Advantage-Maker. You saw how that battle turned out.

If you are not an Advantage-Maker, odds are you will likely lose to a leader who is.

For 23 years, I've been working with extraordinary leaders. I've noticed that some leaders almost always find the right path. They turn situations to their best advantage by seeing possibilities that others don't see.

I call these rare leaders *Advantage-Makers*.

The Advantage-Maker's Skills

An increased means of accomplishing their aims:

- Get the most out of what they have
- Spot opportunities others don't even know exist
- Influence situations to achieve superior outcomes
- The timing to be the go-to person in high-stakes business challenges

Superior effectiveness in midst of constraints:

- The pragmatic ability to make the hard decisions
- Learn more, faster, and course-correct from mistakes quicker
- Design structures that succeed

Harness people's ingenuity:

- Tactical strategies to resolve recurrent conflicts
- Collaborate to create breakaway strategies
- The power to persuade difficult people

Advantage-Makers are pathfinders who anticipate patterns, advance their organizations, and get the most out of everything they have. They learn more, learn more quickly, and develop breakaway strategies. Their healthy skepticism helps them spot difficulties that they transform into opportunities. Most of all, they have the heart of a lion when facing adversity.

These attributes are not accidental. They are hard-won skills. I've discovered over decades that they are teachable and learnable. In fact, successful people have many of them already— they just need to amplify them. The more successful the person, the more leveraged the improvement.

Advantage-Makers' skill, advantage-making, consistently creates superior outcomes in the face of constraints. Resources are leveraged in simple, timely solutions that might not have been initially obvious. If you are not an Advantage-Maker, you likely will be outmaneuvered by someone who is.

Seeing Strategic Opportunities

What enables Advantage-Makers to see strategic opportunities that others overlook? Advantage-Makers are able to strategically shift to find commanding vantage points. **Strategic shifting** is adopting the right angle, the most useful perspective(s), to see a situation and maximize opportunity.

From the higher ground of a **commanding vantage point,** leaders are able to

- Read complex situations
- Take advantage of constantly changing, dynamic circumstances
- Spot opportunities that others can't see from their more limited vantage points

■   Establish a superior strategy, a favorable situation, or a profitable course of action

Leaders with the penetrating insight and sound judgment of an Advantage-Maker are able to turn everything to their best possible advantage while guarding against the designs of their competitors.

Whatever outcomes you are achieving, the perspective of the Advantage-Maker helps you create a superior outcome.

The advantage-making strategies can be applied to an array of management challenges:

Strategic

■   Do more with less, faster
■   Enrich strategic thinking and decision making
■   Create strategies for business growth

Organizational

■   Build a team of Advantage-Makers
■   Fix interdepartmental and collaboration conflicts
■   Design the underlying performance structures to be more effective
■   Create momentum and correct lack of alignment

Leadership

■   Direct a major change
■   Improve leadership influence and effectiveness
■   Boost performance of newly promoted executives
■   Pull your—or someone else's—feet out of the fire

As a leader, whether you need to beat the odds or take advantage of an opportunity, the consequences are significant for you and your organization. You either create an advantage or react from a disadvantage.

Advantage-Makers do the right thing to spot opportunities, create advantages, and influence outcomes.

Do the Right Thing

"Do the right thing."

That's what my Dad encouraged me to do when making decisions or handling any difficulty.

Because clues were not always immediately clear and the standards for "the right thing" were ambiguous, I didn't know the right thing to do each time—or, for that matter, what doing the right thing meant. The good news was that this ambiguity led me on a search. *The bad news was that at times I took my limited experience as the limits of the world.* Many of us make this mistake. Positioning yourself at a constructive vantage point increases the likelihood of seeing things clearly and making the right judgment.

The Eighth Floor

A manager from Sun Microsystems, located in the San Francisco Bay Area, was trying to grasp the meaning and implication of seeing things from the right vantage point. We were on the eighth floor of a ten-story building. Walking over to the window, we looked out over all the traffic on Highway 101 and the surrounding neighborhoods. It was 5:30 p.m., and the surge of workers heading home was predictably clogging the highway's on-ramps and slowing traffic into that aggravating crawl we've ironically dubbed "rush hour." One blue Toyota, in particular, caught our attention. Its driver was trying to work his way around the jam by using surface streets. He was doing a good job until he made a left turn, no doubt thinking it would be a shortcut.

Unfortunately, he couldn't see that this "shortcut" would make his trip much longer, because he would be heading straight into a construction zone. From the eighth floor, we had a *commanding vantage point* of the traffic flow. The left turn seemed like a good idea from the view on the ground, but we had the right vantage point to obtain complete information on the traffic.

We've all had such opportunities, when we could see what others couldn't see. Moreover, such an opportunity isn't just one person's opinion, point of view, or perspective. It comes from being in a commanding position from which you can rapidly see the condition of "traffic," the reality of the situation, the interactions of the parties involved, the forces at play, and the tendency for movement, which can all result in making the right judgment.

No doubt at times you felt you had a commanding vantage point. Why don't you have a commanding vantage point all the time, or even most of the time? What keeps us from getting to the eighth floor and looking out that window?

Our driver was burdened by more than the traffic jam. First, he interpreted his circumstance based upon his selective perception—that is, through the filters of his background, experiences, attitudes, and interests. His selective perception helped him to read the situation quickly, but it narrowed his comprehension of what he was actually up against.

Second, the driver picked the first solution that seemed "good enough"—making the choice based on limited information.[2] This lightning-fast mental process leads to constructing simplistic and, at times, limiting models that might not capture the actual situation. "It seemed like a good idea at the time" is a common refrain.

When faced with a problem, people reduce it to a manageable level and find solutions that are not too far from the status quo, much as the driver did when he took the first possible turn off a crowded road. It was a possible solution to the problem of slow traffic, but from the eighth floor, it was clear that the first solution was far from being right. Advantage-Makers take an eighth-floor view—when it comes to business problems, they do not stop at the first possible solution—instead they immediately look at the bigger picture.

The behavioral tendency to choose the first solution can create a real cost for you. If you base your decisions on the order in which solutions arrive, what if the solution you choose increases your business slightly, but the next option—the one you did not consider—would double your effectiveness, your yield, or your market size? You would be leaving a lot of money on the table.

I'm not suggesting that you make an exhaustive list of all the options every time you make a decision. Gut feelings can reflect the wisdom of experience. Sometimes it really is appropriate to go with your first gut decision and rapidly course-correct.

If we, on the eighth floor, had a communication system, we could have sent the right information at the right time to help the driver. In reality, had he turned right instead of left, he would have made faster progress. In many situations, having good scouts is critical to making informed decisions.

Getting information in a timely fashion can make a significant difference; it can change a loss into an opportunity. Many of us make the error of shutting off information or limiting our judgment to what we can see based upon our own past experience. This is a huge mistake.

Positioning Yourself at the Appropriate Vantage Point Fosters Clear Judgment

Advantage-making leaders strategically shift to commanding vantage points to see opportunities, create advantages, and influence outcomes.

A commanding vantage point is a targeted viewpoint from which leaders can

- "Read" the situation—the expected and unexpected patterns of dynamic interactions and perceptions among people, groups, and organizations
- Shift their own perceptions, decisions, and behaviors as needed so that their positions are as dynamic as the environment

Advantage-Makers are the rare leaders who have mastered the art of *strategic shifting*. By shifting their focus and finding the best vantage point from which to look at a problem, they maximize opportunity and shift the odds in their favor.

Strategic Shifting

The first critical element in strategic shifting is finding a commanding vantage point, such as a strategic hill, from which to look at a situation and see reality clearly. Commanding vantage points can be dynamic and provide an edge. How do leaders shift to commanding vantage points? Knowing the appropriate shift to make is critical to success—for example, a shift from thinking that a situation is a "people" issue, when, in fact, it is a business strategy issue. Strategic shifting is dynamically adapting to the right position.

To survive and thrive, attention and control should go to the person with the best knowledge and capability in a particular situation. Command is not about ordering people around because you are a superior. It's about having command over the issues. As the landscape changes and uncertainty increases, the odds shift in your favor by the quality of your responses to what is most relevant and urgent.

Strategic shifting is anchored in the behavioral sciences and confirmed in the real world of leadership, organizational performance, and business achievement. The insights of strategic shifting are based upon analyzing the interaction of behaviors and positions in everyday encounters. By detecting productive and counterproductive maneuvers, organizational Advantage-Makers can recommend strategic interactions that have a higher probability of working. Strategic shifting is a model for acting and moving. It provides maneuverability—agility of mind, ability to change course, ingenuity of strategy, and skill in creating forward movement.

We examine interactions between people, between groups, between organizations, and between companies. An important factor is assessing the forces that drive behavior. Behavior is dynamic. Seeing is not enough. Dynamic environments require dynamic shifts that match the scope of the problems you encounter.

Strategic shifting reveals blind spots, reactive tendencies, and weaknesses, as well as places of strength, and leverage for leaders and their organizations. When you see the reality you are up against—the good, the bad, and the ugly—you can employ advantage-making strategies to leverage your resources and find opportunities. This propels your strategic influence, shifting the odds in your favor.

Strategic Shifting at Work

Bill Fields, President of Packaging Results, was facing a difficult business environment and needed to produce more revenue. The sales reps complained that they were not able to get in to see prospects. Customer acquisition strategies weren't working.

As Bill stepped back to examine both his thought process and the actions his team was implementing, he noticed an entire dynamic in the business channel that was being overlooked—manufacturer relationships. He looked at the channel further to determine which companies could support his organization's capabilities. These manufacturers were major players in the packaging industry—their targets were big customers. Packaging Results, a distributor, handled the smaller customers. He asked himself, "How do I leverage their sales force, advertising, marketing, website, and industry strength?" From this new vantage point, he could see how these large manufacturers could help his company acquire the accounts. He had cultivated relationships with them for several years and now approached them with a marketing plan to show how they could affiliate together. The manufacturers weren't structured to support these smaller customers, but through the affiliation, they could increase their sales volume and achieve higher margins. Packaging Results would take the leads the manufacturers didn't want because those small companies were outside the manufacturers' focus.

A Profitable Course of Action

This approach achieved two things for Bill. First, he increased his number of customers. Second, he received pricing concessions that he wouldn't have acquired in any other way. In fact, competitors never received these prices. A more conventional way would have been to hire more salespeople and pay for more advertising—the normal things in the selling process that are part of the sales expense. Instead, this partnership produced more gross profit and sales. His selling expense went down, the cost of acquiring prospects decreased, and the sales force was more productive.

This shift produced $500,000 of increased business in the first year alone, plus there was a residual impact going forward. When Bill built value for customers, the average customer life cycle was 5–8 years; multiply that by $500,000 over the time frame, and you have $2.5–$4 million residual business. On top of that, the approach produced back-end sales for additional materials customers purchased. One final advantage was the referrals he would create from satisfying these new customers.

A major growth opportunity was found where none was even possible before. Bill and his team won the new accounts in a win-win-win gain for customers, the manufacturer, and his company.

Though the idea of using partners is not new, this everyday example illustrates how a smart businessperson can get mired in linear thinking—"the shortest point between me and the customer is knocking on the customer's door."

Opportunity Eyes

Your situation will likely be different from Bill's. However, what is equally relevant and urgent is the quality of your advantage-making skills. The principle of strategic shifting can lead you to a profitable course of action. Not having a commanding vantage point reduces success rates, and not being able to strategically shift at the right time reduces success rates dramatically.

Bill is not new to creating unexpected advantages. The key for him is to look at his own business and then search for ideas and connections in neighboring industries. He examines the network of interactions in the distribution channel; this takes him beyond his narrowly focused immediate objective. Looking at these industries allows him to step out of his daily grind and see how others operate. Once out of his mental rut, he can shift to look at his own business with "opportunity eyes." Shifting enables him to see as an outsider, a vital ability because breakthrough thinking often comes from the outside.

The Advantage-Maker's Independent Stance Is Paramount for Sound Judgment

The outsider's vantage point welcomes possibility. For example, Pasteur was not a medical doctor, and the airplane-inventing Wright brothers were bicycle mechanics.

Going against prevailing wisdom takes courage. At times, the underdog Advantage-Makers need to battle for credibility, similar to Galileo standing up to the medieval church's geocentric view that the sun revolved around the earth.

Preconceived notions can misguide you. Strategic shifting presents rules of thumb that serve as shortcuts. It answers questions such as these:

- In searching for an advantage, which vantage points provide the most leverage?
- In resolving difficult performance issues, how does persistence become counterproductive instead of helping you fix the problem—and what to do to succeed?
- To increase your leadership efficacy, when is adaptability more powerful than force?
- To reduce the likelihood that your change effort will fail (65% of such efforts fail[3]), how can you identify

the real conflicts and the biggest sources of leverage that many executives miss?

■   What is the first principle that every great strategic influencer employs to avoid bungling an opportunity?

Not all leaders are Advantage-Makers. If you apply *any* of the commanding vantage points in this book on an as-needed basis, you can become a better leader. However, this is not just another leadership book. It introduces four Advantage Points that, if mastered, will make you an Advantage-Maker.

Advantage-Makers shift between strategic moves and tactical angles, between confronting objective reality and influencing perceptions to create reality, between the expected and the unexpected, between using the rules and creating new rules, between employing big forces at play and using the small but relevant distinctions that make a difference.

Advantage-Makers see leadership as a high leverage point for influence and impact. Advantage-making is a craft that masterful leaders employ. Whatever shift is required, they make it, and they find an edge to create leverage.

Good Judgment

A young man goes to a successful Advantage-Maker and asks, "How did you get such good business judgment?"

"Through experience," replies the Advantage-Maker.

"Where did you get the experience?" the young man asks, excited to get an answer.

"Through poor judgment!" muses the Advantage-Maker.[4]

The moral of this little story is that there's wisdom to be acquired from mistakes—but there's no need for *you* to make all the mistakes; you can instead learn from the experiences of others. This book explains how poor judgment occurs and how to avoid or minimize missteps. It includes examples of poor judgments made by leaders, strategists, and advisors (including my own mistakes).

It examines errors and failures that have occurred over the years. It is a composite of what not to do, counterproductive action, and the poor advice others have offered to leaders and managers.

It is written for real people, with real jobs, who want to create real results. It is not for impostors or do-it-yourself know-it-alls who keep repeating what they already know, whether it fits or not.

If this book were only about poor judgments, you wouldn't want, or need, to read it. The daily newspaper is full of mistakes made by managers and especially government officials, and everyone who works in an office has opinions of how managers mess up and what they would do differently, given the chance. Being a critic is easy. Coming up with a novel solution is much harder.

We examine how leaders handle and mishandle difficulties. Finding yourself between a rock and a hard place is not uncommon within the executive suite. Creating advantage in times of uncertainty requires at least one added dimension. This book identifies four *Advantage Points* to aid you in finding hidden opportunities.

A Missing Dimension

Many managers are experienced and capable, but not yet masterful. A master is someone who has a comprehensive grasp of all the nuances in his field. On any given day, a person may inadvertently bungle an opportunity, possibly because he or she just doesn't know that things could be done differently. Renowned social psychologist Dr. Robert Cialdini put it this way: "Bunglers of influence are ethical people who don't know that there are ways to do things more effectively. They miss the opportunities that are right in front of them."[5]

We can find opportunities that we might otherwise miss by examining previously overlooked dimensions or by looking at situations from new angles. The cost of lost opportunity can come in the form of revenue and expenses—even careers.

In my experience, even the most capable people have blind spots; they bungle opportunities because the solutions that are workable never occur to them. Fortunately, this partial blindness is curable, not terminal.

An Added Dimension

In the famous story *The Hound of the Baskervilles,* Sherlock Holmes is investigating a crime scene at a large home.[6] During his interviews with witnesses, he discovers something peculiar: The dog in the home hadn't barked during the break-in. This seemingly unimportant fact captures his attention. While others round up the usual suspects, this mysterious clue engages Holmes. The answer to who had committed the crime becomes evident to him as he reviews the evidence. Because the dog normally barked at strangers, Holmes deduces that the dog must have known the culprit. It was an inside job.

Most of us solve problems by rounding up the usual suspects. Holmes looked where others didn't. His solutions to crimes were there to be seen by anyone who knew how to look and listen. Holmes heard what was being said, as well as what wasn't said (or wasn't barked), and contrasted the two. Solving mysteries in true Holmesian fashion is an excellent example of dimensional thinking. Holmes was not linear in his approach; he was versatile in shifting his attention to different dimensions of a problem.

Many experienced detectives would have missed the clue of the silent dog even though it was obvious in hindsight. People are trained to look at what's *there* (and are not always so well trained in that), not at what is *absent*. Similarly, many experienced executives miss opportunities that are right in front of them. With a hectic, get-it-done, accelerated pace, they tend to be linear in their approach. They aren't thinking dimensionally—that is, shifting their vantage point to see hidden opportunity. As a consequence, their primary efforts remain operational and tactical rather than strategic.

This book provides you with a framework for advantage-making. Applying the commanding vantage points outlined in these chapters should shift the odds in your favor. Just like the fortress commander, seeing possibilities that others don't know to look for creates a real edge. By making penetrating insights and sound judgments, you turn everything to your best possible advantage and guard against the designs of others. This is the foundation for creating superior outcomes.

The Advantage-Maker's Advice

Leadership is the province of getting it right.
Anyone who tells you differently hasn't been in a position of leadership.
You don't need to know all the answers.
You do need to know how to create solutions.
Mishandling difficulties puts you at a further disadvantage.
How do you shift the odds in your favor? Hint: Shift.
For further explanation, see Chapter 2, "Breaking the Secret Code of the Great Advantage-Makers."

Chapter Recap

1. Advantage-Makers turn everything to their best possible advantage and create superior outcomes.
2. Advantage-Makers are able to design choices that others don't even know exist.
3. If you are not an Advantage-Maker, odds are you will lose to a leader who is.
4. Strategic shifting is adopting the right angle, and an added dimension, to maximize opportunity and shift the odds in your favor.
5. A commanding vantage point is like a strategic hill from which to look at situations and see reality clearly. Commanding vantage points can be dynamic; they provide an edge.

Endnotes

1. Paul Watzlawick, John Weakland, and Richard Fisch, *Change: Principles of Problem Formation and Problem Resolution* (New York, N.Y.: Norton, 1974).

2. Herbert Simon, *Administrative Behavior*, 3d ed. (New York: The Free Press, 1976). Simon describes this kind of thinking as bounded rationality; another related concept is *satisficing* (a combination of *satisfying* and *sufficing*).

3. Pierre Mourier and Martin Smith, *Conquering Organizational Change: How to Succeed Where Most Companies Fail* (New York, N.Y.: CEP Press, 2001).

    B. J. Bashein, M. I. Markus, and Patricia Riley, "Preconditions for BPR Success and How to Prevent Failure," *Information Systems Management* 11, no. 2 (1994): 7–13.

Meta Group, Gartner Group, and Cap Gemini E&Y indicate that CRM initiatives fail 50%–90% of the time.

4. As seen on a cubicle office at Sun Microsystems.

5. Robert Cialdini in describing his "Principles of Persuasion."

6. Sir Arthur Conan Doyle, *The Hound of the Baskervilles* (New York: Grosset & Dunlap, 1902).

CHAPTER 2

Breaking the Secret Code of the Great Advantage-Makers

I'm not trying to copy Nature. I'm trying to find the principles she is using.

—R. Buckminster Fuller

Advantage-Makers are those rare leaders who win more often than others by transforming challenging situations into the best possible outcomes. They see opportunities where others see only problems, influence outcomes where others are stuck, and create advantages where others are challenged.

Their skill, advantage-making, is designed to consistently create superior outcomes in the face of constraints. Good timing and simple solutions leverage assets in surprising ways.

Have you ever felt you were going 90 miles per hour in your car and had to change the tires while moving? That's exactly how the CIO of Wells Fargo, Barry X Lynn, described his world to me. Merging Wells Fargo and First Interstate Bank required integrating two entirely different systems without shutting down daily banking business. They accomplished the task in eight months. The industry standard was more than 30 months. The key was not how fast they were able to work, but how fast they were able to make decisions and move forward. In some cases, the correct decision was not perfectly clear, but as Barry said, "Rather than analyze the alternatives to death, we chose moving on to the next step."[1]

With this forward movement, he shifted the resources to align the team, creating an unusually high level of focus—rapidly adapting, almost as if he could see around corners. In the face of this daunting task, Barry treated people with dignity, and his command presence inspired confidence to find solutions.

Constraints

Constraints are a fact for any business. The opposite of leverage, constraints hold back or limit the potential outcome. They can affect the organization's purpose of creating, maintaining, and growing customers. Availability of resources is often a limiting factor. Advantage-Makers recognize this challenge but might be the first to see that the real problem is in how people are using their scarce resources.

Constraints vary from the ordinary to the extreme. Limits to development, progress, or improvement are common conditions Advantage-Makers face. Beyond budget and supply and demand issues, limits might be imposed by:

- Competition, with price and barriers to entry
- Organizational design, with organizational silos and lack of alignment
- Naturally occurring factors, such as locations and geography
- Time, with delivery schedules, growing seasons, and holiday periods
- Execution challenges, including talent shortages, inefficiencies, or workload outstripping resource capacity
- Government limits, with regulations and legislation

Advantage-Makers don't ignore constraints. They are keenly aware of any limiting factor. They spot it almost when they walk in the door. Advantage-Makers, such as Barry X Lynn, look at constraints as part of their advantage-making materials, similar to the way artists might view their canvas or sculptors might view their stone. They engage the constraint, consciously or unconsciously, putting it to the best possible use.

In general, they do more with less, and do it faster. They often see constraints as motivation for action. Telling Advantage-Makers "No one can do this" or "It's impossible" is a sure way to grab their attention—not because they believe in the impossible, but because they hear opportunity knocking.

In a conversation about constraints, Darrin Caddes, Vice President of Industrial Design at Plantronics, said, "Constraints are not just part of the game; without them there is no game—otherwise, anyone could do it."

Employees at an all-hands meeting asked their CEO about competitive threats to the company. Acknowledging the difficulty confronting them, the CEO said, "I'm not worried about being at a disadvantage; in fact, I've always found that disadvantages sharpen the mind and hone your thinking to make things even better. This company has survived and thrived in the face of adversity before and we will win again, and here is how we are going to do it…." He then provided a plan of action. This wasn't spin; it was a window into the working mind of an Advantage-Maker. The CEO and company had a track record of transforming challenging situations into wins. Constraints actually trigger advantage-making behavior.

Constraints make the game engaging. Advantage-Makers are not looking for trouble; they are not looking to make things hard. On the contrary, they look at constraints and handle them in a way that differentiates them from the rest of the crowd.

Would Anyone Ever Think Number 2 Is a Winner?

Car-rental company Avis is the proud creator of the successful advertising slogan "We're number 2. We try harder!" Avis was failing and on the verge of bankruptcy. The Hertz company was unquestionably number 1 in the marketplace. Avis couldn't compete head-to-head. In lieu of that competition, Avis designed a brilliant strategy that contrasted the focus it put on customer service with that of its competitors. It delivered the "We're number 2. We try harder" message in TV ads, in all its promotional materials, and at airports as passengers walked out to get their cars. Customers loved it and rented more cars from Avis.

What enabled Avis, in particular, and Advantage-Makers, in general, to see strategic opportunities that others overlook?

It's *not* the conventional wisdom that motivational speakers like to promote:

It's not just *tenacity*.	It's not being *unafraid of failure*.
It's not *thinking outside the box*.	It's not *people skills* and *team building*.
It's not *inquisitiveness*.	It's not *delivering on the hard decisions*.
It's not being a *quick learner*.	
It's not being *smarter*.	It's not the proverbial *"bias for action."*
It's not being more *creative*.	

Although good managers exhibit these behaviors, they're not enough. Something is missing.

In fact, each of these behaviors, attitudes, and competencies might be overused or become a rut. Beyond insight, practicality, and common sense, Advantage-Makers act from a strategically advantageous level.

What Strategic Shifts Does the Advantage-Maker Employ?

Advantage-Makers are architects of opportunity. They use four levers:

1. Time
2. Interaction
3. Perception
4. Structure

Strategically shifting these four levers creates an economy of means for producing superior outcomes.

- Shifting time generates possibilities.
- Shifting interaction transforms the game.
- Shifting perception creates winners.
- Shifting structure changes behavior.

The Four Levers: T.I.P.S.

Time

This is *when*—your *time frames (past, present, future)*. Advantage-Makers are highly attuned to the times they live in. They are sensitive to cultural forces. This is not about telling time, keeping time, or building clocks; it's about sensing the right time. Their timing has a directional quality. They combine targets and timing to make sure they are going in the right direction. Timing enables them to keep their eyes on the prize. Getting the timing right is the crux of many advantages and opportunities.

Advantage-Makers can shift their time orientation to the past, present, and future. Their dictum is: There is no time like the present to create the future. Looking far into the future, they can imagine possibilities beyond today.

Imagine that you can travel along a timeline and look back from the future to see the present. Now imagine a wide, panoramic timeline that can move in multiple directions rather than a single, narrow line. Expanding or shortening your timeline can change your emotional state and affect your degrees of freedom.

Advantage-Makers' time awareness enables them to spot and resolve issues early. Changing the time variable in a negotiation can open or shut down options. Advantage-Makers use time to highlight possibilities that others haven't noticed.

Interaction

This is *how* you live—the *pattern of interactions.* An interaction vantage point enables you to see actions not in isolation, but between players. Seeing the pattern of relationships between people, teams, organizations, or companies is the critical link for thinking strategically. The interaction vantage point is a distinctive view that enables you to think differently. To maneuver your way successfully in difficult situations, look closely at people's actions and reactions. Are you taking action when you don't need to, or not taking action when you should?

Furthermore, your conversations may be reactive rather than strategic. Notice how you think about situations and how that translates into the communication and conversations you have with others.

Advantage-Makers are game changers who master interaction plays that others don't expect. Expect the unexpected.

Perception

This is *where* you live—your *mind-sets*. You see what you see. Moreover, what you see—your perceptions—drives behavior. Clear observations can produce penetrating insights. However, perceptual biases can interfere with seeing reality clearly. As a result, you miss possibilities for the enterprise as well.

Fundamentally, leaders are perceivers. Being an effective leader, influencing others, and seeing possibilities where others don't require strategic perceptions. Winners see things differently; they orient toward outcomes and approach situations proactively. Winners see options, whereas losers complain. Advantage-Makers learn and grow rather than already know. Keenly aware of influencing perceptions, Advantage-Makers frame arguments to impact decisions. When you can see, you can act.[2] Seeing as an Advantage-Maker, you can act as an Advantage-Maker.

Structure

This is the *invisible why* in your life—*the driving form*, the forces at work that cause you to do what you do. To understand behavior in business, let's consider behavior in nature. Rivers are dynamic, yet they have predictable paths. What causes a river's predictable pattern? The water follows the underlying structure of the riverbed. Just as a riverbed determines the river's course of action, your business has an underlying structure that determines its course of action—profitable or otherwise. Structural dynamics developed by Robert Fritz clarify how structure drives behavior.[3] Unrecognized, the structural forces can neutralize your best efforts and are a main reason change efforts fail. Orchestrating the structural forces can achieve advantages where previously there were disadvantages.

Objective structures can include rewards, market forces, competition, buying motivation, objectives, decisions, policies, and communication strategies. Design the structure for success. For example, aligning objectives, decision authority, and rewards with the customer and market establishes the performance structure for forward movement.

Industry structural changes in financial services, retail and distribution, and health care touch our lives in our work and as consumers. The Internet structurally changed our lives.

Similarly, your subjective experience has an underlying form, a structure of subjective experience, as described by Richard Bandler and John Grinder.[4] Change the structure, and you change your behavior.

Advantage-making is a set of internal elements that, woven together, form a structure that creates leverage. Think as an Advantage-Maker thinks—for example, "use dissatisfaction constructively"—and you begin developing options. Without this emotional framework of using dissatisfaction constructively, you can become cynical and miss opportunities.

Advantage-Makers leverage time to influence outcomes, interactions to transform the game, perceptions to create winners, and the structures to drive behavior. Now let's return to the Avis example and see the significant shifts that enabled Avis to succeed in the midst of failing efforts.

Avis Shifts the Game

With troubles in the marketplace, it was *time to shift*. It was unlikely that Avis could have achieved its turnaround without strategic shifting. Momentum was going in the wrong direction. Resolving the challenges facing the company was essential. Avis began a process of *architecting a different future*.

The single biggest perception shift Avis made was to *see that the attempted solution*—a head-to-head battle with Hertz—was a nonproductive pattern that would lead to bankruptcy.

Many advisors will tell you, "If what you are doing isn't working, do something different." Great advice, but how? And what specifically should you be doing differently? Avis examined what it was doing and must have asked a seemingly innocuous and obvious question: "How is it working?" Although it is often asked, this question might lead to nonobvious but fruitful solutions if you know how to look and what to look for.

Many solutions to intransigent problems lie in examining the conventions and applying *unexpected strategies on the conventions*. First, you need to look at your attempted solutions[5] for clues to what shouldn't be done anymore. Then, from the same information comes an equally important shift, the shift to see new directions—that is, to do something different.

Avis certainly worked hard. However, Hertz's barriers were too strong—they were number 1. Up to the point of bankruptcy, Avis's attempted solution was to work harder trying to be number 1.

Then Avis shifted; it made the unexpected claim that it was number 2. The conventional mind-set is to always want to be recognized as the winner. Positioning your company as an also-ran, number 2, is certainly not an easy shift, but Avis's success, in part, is attributable to this shift. How did they generate the shift?

Avis's attempted solutions, in both mind-sets and business strategy, dismissed the fact that the company couldn't catch up. The business turnaround was preceded by *180° conceptual turnaround*, a mental shift of not fighting the runner-up status. It took brave leadership to take that step. Avis realized that its previous attempted solutions wouldn't work. Rather than persisting with more of the same strategy, Avis attacked its frozen, repetitive efforts. Furthermore, the company didn't do a false marketing job on itself—it confronted reality. No one wants to admit to being number 2, but to Avis's credit, by doing so, the company spotted an opportunity that most would miss.

Avis shifted 180°—it broadcast its "failure." Hertz was number 1, and Avis was number 2. But Avis obviously didn't stop there. Influence research shows that *when you argue against your self-interest, you are immediately seen as trustworthy, and the next thing you say will be viewed as credible*[6]—"We try harder." Customers' perceptions moved from "We are not interested in Avis" to "They try harder—Avis is for me." This advertising campaign further shifted a fundamental principle of influence known as the *contrast principle.* Contrasting their efforts with Hertz's captured the imagination of rental car drivers.

Avis required one more shift—to structure the organization to succeed. The company needed to align behavior with the new business strategy. This is an important point because, on average, 65% of change efforts fail.[7] They fail because the underlying structure doesn't support the desired behavior. The underlying structure is not in plain sight—it requires looking deeply at how the local decisions are being made inside the organization. Avis needed to free up employees' interactions with customers; their decisions couldn't be hampered by bureaucracy. By all accounts, that's just what they did. Frontline personnel could actually go the extra mile to help customers. Avis *aligned the organization's performance structure* and reward system to support the "Avis: We're number 2. We try harder!" campaign. The organization was structured to succeed as "number 2." From bankruptcy to number 2, we try harder. And Avis did.

None of these advantages would have been accomplished if Avis hadn't employed skillful strategic shifting. Advantage-Makers turn everything to their best advantage by seeing possibilities that others don't see. Finding the right shift seems like magic, but a method to the madness actually exists. Employing the shifts enables you to achieve unexpected gains. This rigorous advantage-making framework has enabled many managers to become Advantage-Makers.

Let's take a closer look at the actual hidden Code of the Advantage-Maker. Barry X Lynn at Wells Fargo employed these shifts to go 90 miles per hour, change the tires while moving, and still create superior outcomes.

The Code of the Advantage-Maker

Advantage-Makers dynamically adapt to the right position. They adopt the right angle to maximize opportunity by employing unique operating principles.

A. Time Shifts

1. Architect the Future

Advantage-Makers believe that there is no time like the present to create the future. Their first act is to define how the future should look. Their approach is to imagine what could be, listen for the buzz to questions they have, and gravitate to forward movement. As pathfinders, they anticipate patterns and the playing field—to position their organizations to win. Their eyes are often on possible futures, and their actions are on shaping the future. They love creating the future.

On his deathbed, Walt Disney described to a journalist an imaginary yet detailed map of a future Disney World. It seemed like a fanciful reverie of a dying man. Years later, Disney World and Epcot Center were completed. Someone said, "Isn't it a shame he never lived to see his idea realized?" One of Disney's creative people answered, "But he did see it—that's why it's here."[8]

Right now, Google is creating the future. Google's founders, Larry Page and Sergey Brin, are connection-makers who are a step ahead in anticipating and shaping the future.

2. Manage Momentum

Advantage-Makers orchestrate rapid forward movement, capitalizing on momentum and advancing the organization by aligning the performance structure. As momentum players, they have command over the phased movement of a project. They are always thinking of the next move. Doing the right thing at the right time is what matters to them. Advantage-Makers find the single biggest factor to leverage, whether it is within the individual, team, organization, or business. They are particularly attuned to the power of inertia to keep things moving forward. When they find it, they rapidly shift that dynamic to create a profitable course of action.

Starbucks CEO Howard Schultz capitalized on "experience retailing"—people want their Starbucks—and built momentum so that every neighborhood has a Starbucks. Undeniably, Starbucks has changed the way we drink coffee.

Marv Tseu, Chairman of the Board for Plantronics, the leading provider of headsets, intentionally creates forward move-ment with the appropriate growth investments. Collaborating with Plantronics CEO Ken Kannappan, they constantly scan for the next innovation to get ahead of the curve in B2B and consumer markets.

3. Use Time Strategically

Advantage-Makers are time sensors. They sense time the way other people sense emotion. Similar to others, they think about the past, present, and future. However, they think about them in distinctive ways. The time horizon for Advantage-Makers can range from 1 day to 25 years—or much longer. Additionally, Advantage-Makers recognize that decisions can shift, depending upon whether they are paying attention to the past, present, or future. Sensing the significance of each of those time frames, they choose. Their choice steers them toward a resolution.

Many people think that their past causes what is happening or will happen to them; others think that what they do in the present will create the future. When Advantage-Makers are advantage-making, they think into the future and think backward. That is, the future can change the next step. While being responsive to the present, they recognize that the future guides them. And not only do they think that the future can cause the present, but in their language, you can hear how the future will cause further future changes. Time is a language, and Advantage-Makers are fluent in the language of time.

Penny Herscher, Chairwoman and CEO of Simplex Solutions, an electronic design automation company, continuously focuses on the endgame and compels her people to keep the future in mind when making decisions. This multiplies the value of everyone's efforts.

At BEA Systems, CIO Jim Haar successfully manuevers toward the future. He navigates resource constraints and too many projects by making tactical moves for short-term requirements, adjusting the time horizon—one week, three months, one year, and so on. As a tactical strategist, he establishes a hierarchy of importance and then reprioritizes and reorders projects to contribute to the business result.

4. *Anticipate and Resolve Issues Early*

Good timing is a hallmark of Advantage-Makers. They scan situations, sense the significance of issues, and sense the right time to deal with them. To guide people to see the difficult things that matter most, Advantage-Makers are early resolvers, but not too early. Timing is so critical to the way they operate that their sense of direction and sense of time are intricately connected. Going in the wrong direction unsettles them. If the targets they select are wrong, they get early warning signals that they must do something different.

While the future is compelling for Advantage-Makers, paradoxically, the present is active. Now is the time to create solutions. Now is the time to move in the right direction. Now is the opportunity.

Y. Y. Lee, Executive Vice President of Operations at firstRain, a premium search-based platform providing in-depth financial and corporate intelligence for institutional investors, shortens development time by adopting a panoramic view of the present and future to steer divergent teams and resolve difficult technical issues. In advance, she highlights the specific pressures and demands that each functional team and leader will have to put on other teams in trying to solve for their portion of the objectives. This process creates an explicit, open, and highly efficient environment for the teams to tackle the most difficult and ambiguous cross-functional issues. It gives Y.Y. continual visibility into areas of positive progress, unexpected innovation, and where teams are getting stuck. She can then intervene and adjust the strategies and pressures across the teams to accelerate progress.

Timely responsiveness was one of the keys for Jan Carlson, CEO of SAS airlines, to turn the company around from $20 million in the red to $80 million in earnings by managing the significant moments of truth—the points in time when a service impression is made on passengers. It determined repeat business. Without this advantage-making approach, the company would have remained in the red.[9]

B. Interaction Shifts

1. Leverage Interactions

Unexpected leverage exists in the patterns of interaction between people, departments, divisions, customers, and other businesses. Networks of opportunity can be found within these interactions. Witness the Internet. By shifting the patterns, unforeseen solutions are created. Expect the unexpected to change the game.

Advantage-Makers realize that interactions are dynamic. When they aren't getting the desired result, they don't persist in doing more of the same—they do something unexpected. As game changers, Advantage-Makers are masters (like the fortress commander) of interactional plays that others don't expect.

To understand the fate of an organization, you need to understand its relationship to its business environment and culture. Opportunity can be found in the interactions.

In the face of constraints, Ben de Waal, Vice President of Software at NVidia, a leading graphic chip maker, examines recurrent interactions that don't work and replaces them with unexpected tactics that have a higher probability of success. Instead of demanding, he collaborates; instead of telling his fellow executives they have to slow down, he agrees they should go faster—only with a different approach. A game changer, he maneuvers through the present as he architects the future.

Richard Schulze, founder and Chairman of Best Buy, says, "I was at first hesitant to go outside and bring in external know-how. Strategic partnering has now become an extremely important part of how we do business. We now realize we don't have a monopoly on all the ideas."[10]

2. Stretch Your Adaptability Rapidly

Course correction is a governing method for Advantage-Makers. Although they make as many mistakes as others, if not more, they are quicker to correct their course. They recognize defeat as temporary, and they use failure as feedback to suggest course corrections. To achieve this, they are constantly making new links; in effect, they are connection-makers. While keeping their eye on the prize, they don't short-circuit the connections between what they are creating and ideas that previously seemed unrelated. Surprising connections arise, leading to opportunities that don't exist for others. Advantage-Makers are doers, learners, and teachers, not only adapting their own ability but others' as well. They encourage and teach others to rapidly adapt, while supporting and developing their advantage-making skills. The person with the widest range of responses wins. Nonadaptiveness is costly. Flexibility and mental agility instead of force can lead to increasing control.

Current General Electric CEO Jeff Immelt shifts directions and advocates change, ridding the corporation of sacred cows. "Most people inside GE learn from the past but have a healthy disrespect for history. They have an ability to live in the moment and not be burdened by the past, which is extremely important," says Immelt. They rapidly adapt and course-correct effectively.[11]

John Chambers, CEO of Cisco, said at a Stanford Technology Industry Conference, "This is an industry that's like the Indy 500: You are going as fast as you can at times, and then all of a sudden you are in the Tour de France, where you had the turns that you never expected."[12]

3. Collaborate to Design Simplicity into Solutions

Advantage-Makers value simplicity—not simplistic solutions, but elegant, high-leverage solutions. To achieve this, they seek the input of high-performing collaborators, actively inquiring about how others see things differently. To design breakaway strategies, they experiment, collaborate, learn, fail, and rebound more in a shorter amount of time than most everyone else. Surprising solutions arise, leading to opportunities that don't exist for others.

The Wharton Management School honored Dr. Alejandro Zaffaroni with a prestigious award for his major pioneering achievements in biotechnology. As a successful founder of numerous biotechnology companies, he said, "When I look back, I can see many cases where the initial business idea was transformed and something new was created. In great part, my success has been due to all the bright men and women who have collaborated with me."[13]

Wells Fargo Bank became a leading electronic provider of financial services under CIO Barry X. Lynn, who is as much a businessperson as a technologist. Always a student of human behavior, he would drop what wasn't working; his advantage-making tendencies enabled him to find ways to leverage customer interactions. With his people, he created anytime, anywhere connectivity—they connected the laptop, the ATM, the branch teller, and the mainframe computer to a single network.

4. Cultivate Command Presence

Advantage-Makers have the heart of a lion in the face of adversity. They are confident in their own efficacy to create superior outcomes. Even as underdogs, they have command of the issues and of generating solutions. When they engage their full attention, they become a powerful force. It's worth noting that this is not about ordering people around; instead, they are a credible source of influence. Advantage-Makers are perceived by others as having command presence. This contrasts with a reactive, complaining, and blaming mode.

Herb Kelleher, founder and CEO of Southwest Airlines, confidently plays to win, shifting how people perceive airline travel by structuring point-to-point destinations, ticket change policy, roles, responsibilities, and jobs.

C. Perception Shifts

1. Approach Situations Proactively

Advantage-Makers keep their eyes on the prize. They play to win rather than play to avoid losing. Their outcome orientation keeps them targeted on solutions rather than reacting to the circumstances they encounter. In contrast to the proactive approach, a reactive tendency can inadvertently maintain problems, weakening real fixes by concealing or deflecting from what will make a difference.

While Advantage-Makers realize that perception drives behavior, they don't confuse this with the more common, and at times faulty, notion that perception is reality. They take a fresh, unbiased, and independent approach to achieve outcomes. Their method is to objectively look at a problem without prior expectations or predetermined solutions. Curiosity and an intrinsic drive catapult their desires to create differences in the world.

FedEx CEO Fred Smith had an independent way of looking at overnight air package delivery. A C grade in graduate school on a paper describing his hub-and-spoke delivery concept didn't dissuade him, nor did any other challenge.

Richard Branson, Chairman of The Virgin Group, a multibillion-dollar business with approximately 200 companies in more than 30 countries, said, "If Virgin stands for anything, it should be for not being afraid to try out new ideas in new areas." Virgin is run as a series of autonomous businesses so that its managers can make independent decisions.[14]

2. Frame Issues Hierarchically

Advantage-Makers determine what's most important in a situation instead of thinking that everything matters equally. Hierarchical thinking is the crux of what enables people to think and act strategically. Without this ability, they can't prioritize effectively or do more with less.

Advantage-Makers know the difference between big problems and small problems, between what matters and what is just noise. This hierarchical approach is passionately focused, first and foremost, on creating fundamentally superior outcomes— making things fundamentally better.

Former General Electric CEO Jack Welch's business dictum to exit an industry if GE can't be number 1 or number 2 is a clear example of hierarchical thinking in practice.[15]

Confronting reality, Bill Gates, founder of Microsoft and now a leading philanthropist, frames issues based upon what's most important to create successful endeavors.

3. Use Dissatisfaction Constructively

Always seeking an economy of means, Advantage-Makers' healthy skepticism leads them to spot difficulties that they transform into opportunities—thus their optimistic outlook. They are adept at identifying weaknesses, blind spots, reactive tendencies, and biases. This ability to pinpoint what is at stake makes them invaluable. While adversity and dissatisfaction might cause others to become discouraged and cynical, Advantage-Makers shift to creating outcomes. They are also willing to recognize shortcomings in themselves, and rather than overlook them, they see them as opportunities for change.

The Marriott Corporation is guided by founder J. W. Marriott's design to not rest on past successes, but to always find ways to improve the company. Employees challenge themselves before the competition does.

Toyota is thriving, perhaps partly due to their dissatisfaction. Their process is to "presume imperfection," search for problems, and constantly strive for improvement in all phases of car manufacturing.[16] Japanese quality guru Shigeo Shingo says, "Dissatisfaction is the mother of all improvement."

4. Influence Perception

Advantage-Makers proactively frame their communication to influence outcomes. They skillfully shape perceptions, persuading others to see what they are missing. To do so, they master the principles of shifting perception.

Curtis Sasaki, Vice President of Sun Web and an Advantage-Maker at Sun Microsystems, was involved in a tense international government negotiation that had ground to a halt. Strategies that often work were unsuccessful. Intermediaries were ineffective. Repeated attempts to gain alignment led nowhere. Applying the strategic influence materials in this book (see Chapter 8, "Strategic Influence: How to Get People to Say Yes in the Right Way to the Right Things," and Chapter 9, "Influence Perception: Helping People See What They Need to See"), Curtis skillfully influenced the stalled negotiation, transforming it into a multimillion-dollar deal.

D. Structural Shifts

1. Position the Business or Organization to Win

Advantage-Makers hierarchically organize their strategies around market and customer drivers. They recognize the strategic value of the forces that drive business, customer, organizational, team, and individual behavior. When they see the forces at play, they are able to establish a commanding vantage point—a strategic position from which to win.

Game changers such as Steve Jobs, CEO of Apple, do the unexpected with their "think different" slogan and operation. Apple continuously shifts the playing field by moving into markets that others dodge. The iPod is everywhere. Was this market being ignored or not seen, or did Apple see its current markets stagnating and look for new opportunities?

George Silverman of Market Navigation points out it was all of these:

"Apple looked for the ignored and unseen in its search for new opportunities. There were numerous MP3 (digital) players in the marketplace. Sony should have owned the market. What was ignored and unseen was the fact that it was very difficult to manage one's music. The hardware makers were thinking hardware. If you had an MP3 player, you still had trouble locating, buying, downloading, and managing your music library. What Apple did with the iPod was to vertically integrate these operations into a simple, elegant, stylish, easy-to-use system. The product isn't the iPod; it's the whole system: the store, iTunes; the iPod; and even its integration with the Mac. The others saw hardware; Jobs saw system, access, and simplicity."[17]

2. Align the Structure to Produce Outcomes

Advantage-Makers change nonadaptive structures in meaningful ways, not just rearranging the deck chairs on the *Titanic*. Their continual analysis of the underlying performance structure is targeted at producing advantageous behavior and eliminating structural conflict.

When Lou Gerstner, CEO of IBM, took over the reins at IBM, he assessed the problem in the computer industry and, instead of breaking IBM apart, refocused IBM to help the customer with system integration from multiple vendors, without requiring all the elements to be bought from IBM. A dramatic structural shift, from a proprietary technology product company to a customer-centric service company.

Proctor & Gamble integrated ideas from outside partners rather than from only their own developments—a major change from a long tradition of internal development. The initiative to bring in outside ideas could produce organizational conflict, and CEO A.G. Lafley stewarded the shift.[18]

3. Make the Hard Decisions

Advantage-Makers employ the judicious use of their power to make the hard choices rather than allowing conflict to fester. Instead of competing against themselves, they structure deals, negotiate contracts, and align organizations to level the playing field. This protects the organization both inside and outside. The *nerve to decide* (making important, tough calls) should not be confused with an unthinking bias for action.

Advantage-Makers know the rules of the game they are playing, as well as how to appropriately use the rules to help them win. With an eye on the horizon, they can preempt and protect against competitive moves. That said, they are as much challenging themselves as they are beating the competition.

Johnson & Johnson CEO James Burke made the now-legendary recall of all Tylenol products because of a small but deadly product-tampering scare. In contrast, companies are vulnerable and employees are confused when executives don't decide on difficult courses of action.

Andy Grove, Chairman of Intel, shifted the odds in his favor by making the hard decisions. He moved from memory devices to microprocessors, and that turned Intel's fortunes around. Grove gathered the evidence, spotted the pattern, tracked the trends, and combined that with the nerve to decide.

4. Do the Strategic Math on the Situation

Just as the stock market can only go up, stay the same, or go down, there are only a few actual possibilities in any situation that matters. Advantage-Makers anticipate the possible options and their consequences and then design ways to increase their odds. However, they don't rule out possibilities prematurely; in fact, they generate multiple scenarios (the "geometry" of possibilities) to consider. It's essential to go *beyond the givens* and do the math on options that provide unexpected solutions. Certainly, risks are part of advantage-making, and doing the strategic math on the situation is fundamental to structuring effective decisions.

Ken Kec, Executive Vice President of HBO & Co., continuously does the strategic math. In almost every meeting I observed, he articulated the "net net" (final answer) of the situation and then recommended the strategic action his company should follow.

Home Depot, the world's largest home improvement retailer, began after the two founders, Bernie Marcus and Arthur Blank, were fired from the Handy Dan home improvement chain. Their new concept emphasized previously overlooked or minimized customer and market drivers—an advantage-making strategy that in fiscal year 2005 reaped $80 billion in sales.[19]

Consciously or otherwise, strategic shifting contributes to the success and impact of managers. Their advantage-making abilities propel them forward.

Are You an Advantage-Maker?

These factors describe the modeling research on Advantage-Makers. Perhaps you've already evaluated yourself against the Advantage-Makers' Code. Although this code may be out of the Advantage-Makers' awareness, their behavior reveals how they function. Some of the factors are more conscious, such as the paramount importance of making hard decisions to resolve competing objectives and conflicts within the organization.

Evaluate Yourself

Rate yourself on the application of the Advantage-Making factors on a scale of 1–10. Score yourself for each factor: 1 is Rarely; 4 is Sometimes; 7 is Often; and 10 is Always. As best you can, score yourself according to what you actually do, not what you know you should do. The more natural the tendency and the quicker you process the shift, the higher you should score; conversely, the more you struggle and the slower you process the shift, the lower you should score.

Several different ratings might be useful for you to do:

1. Your overall general tendency
2. How others would rate you (peers, boss, customers)
3. Assessment of your team's advantage-making

A. Time shifts

1. Architect the future

1----------2----------3---------4---------5----------6----------7----------8---------9---------10
Rarely   Sometimes   Often   Always

2. Manage momentum

1----------2----------3---------4---------5----------6----------7----------8---------9---------10
Rarely   Sometimes   Often   Always

3. Use time strategically

1----------2----------3---------4---------5----------6----------7----------8---------9---------10
Rarely   Sometimes   Often   Always

4. Anticipate and resolve issues early

1----------2----------3---------4---------5----------6----------7----------8---------9---------10
Rarely   Sometimes   Often   Always

B. Interaction shifts

1. Leverage interactions

1----------2----------3---------4---------5----------6----------7----------8---------9---------10
Rarely   Sometimes   Often   Always

2. Stretch your adaptability rapidly

1----------2----------3---------4---------5----------6----------7----------8---------9---------10
Rarely   Sometimes   Often   Always

3. Collaborate to design simplicity into solutions

1----------2----------3---------4---------5----------6----------7----------8---------9---------10
Rarely   Sometimes   Often   Always

4. Cultivate command presence

1----------2----------3---------4---------5----------6----------7----------8---------9---------10
Rarely   Sometimes   Often   Always

C. Perception shifts

1. Approach situations proactively

1---------2---------3---------4---------5---------6---------7---------8---------9---------10
Rarely   Sometimes   Often   Always

2. Frame issues hierarchically

1---------2---------3---------4---------5---------6---------7---------8---------9---------10
Rarely   Sometimes   Often   Always

3. Use dissatisfaction constructively

1---------2---------3---------4---------5---------6---------7---------8---------9---------10
Rarely   Sometimes   Often   Always

4. Influence perception

1---------2---------3---------4---------5---------6---------7---------8---------9---------10
Rarely   Sometimes   Often   Always

D. Structural shifts

1. Position the business or organization to win

1---------2---------3---------4---------5---------6---------7---------8---------9---------10
Rarely   Sometimes   Often   Always

2. Align the structure to produce outcomes

1---------2---------3---------4---------5---------6---------7---------8---------9---------10
Rarely   Sometimes   Often   Always

3. Make the hard decisions

1---------2---------3---------4---------5---------6---------7---------8---------9---------10
Rarely   Sometimes   Often   Always

4. Do the strategic math on the situation

1---------2---------3---------4---------5---------6---------7---------8---------9---------10
Rarely   Sometimes   Often   Always

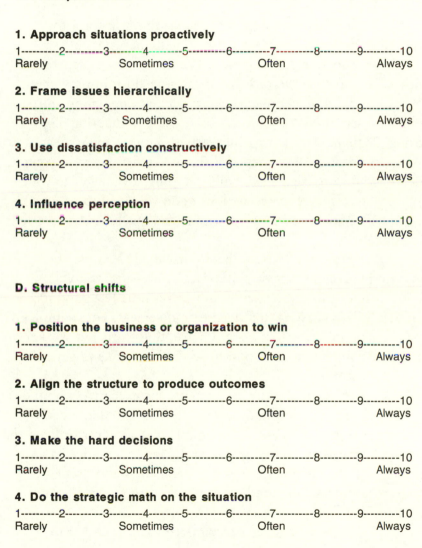

Score Interpretation: A Quick Overview

The scores will point to areas that you want to accentuate as well as improve upon. The highest possible score is 160. 144 is superior, 128 is strong, 112 demonstrates capabilities with some gap areas, 96 or less indicates need for improvement.

Within any one category, such as interaction shifts, your score can total 40 points. A score of 36 is superior, 32 is strong, 28 demonstrates capabilities with improvement areas, and 24 or less needs improvement. With some refinements in your advantage-making skills, you will be adding advantages to your organization. If your scores are lower and you want to be an Advantage-Maker, roll up your sleeves and quickly get to work on the four levers.

How can you use this information? You may be superior in several strategic shifts. Under pressure, you will probably return to these talents, and this is usually a good idea. You might have an area that needs improvement. For example, if you are superior on structural and perception shifts but weaker on interaction shifts, pay attention to your interactions to generate superior outcomes.

After taking the assessment, one executive scored 62%, or 100 out of 160. Although he was a talented leader, specific areas needed improvement. For example he had never realized the power of time as an advantage factor. When he practiced and applied shifting his time frames, he made rapid and dramatic strategic advances. "Astounding" was the word he used for the results.

Another manager recognized that his ability to influence perceptions was low; this was reducing his impact on the organization. Using the ideas from Chapter 9, he began creating advantages and higher-quality outcomes. This rapidly improved his credibility.

How Do the Top Scorers Respond to This Assessment?

Although you might expect people who are talented to think "I know this stuff" and move on, it fascinated me to see that the most powerful Advantage-Makers want to know more to refine their skills. As they reviewed the Code, their results jumped to the next level. Upon a moment's reflection, this makes sense, because Advantage-Makers' inquiry is deep and course correction is rapid.

Your scores are a useful base. You can advance your advantage-making skills by applying the four Advantage Points described in the chapters ahead. Each chapter provides tools to amplify your advantage-making capacity.

Have Others Evaluate You

Ask others to rate you either factor by factor or in general: "Do you think I am an Advantage-Maker?" The words might be different, but the gist of the question is understood. Would they recommend you for a position because of your advantage-making abilities?

Making the Shifts

How to make the most important shifts:

1. Look at a recurrent, persistent problem or challenge.
2. Identify your attempted solutions.
3. Evaluate how the attempted solution is working.
4. Determine the outcome: Either it's working effectively and the problem is solved, or it's not.
5. If it's not, it's time to shift to something *really different*.

Here are beginning exercises to start shifting time, interactions, perceptions, and structures. These four exercises are meant to prime the pump while you think of advantage-making solutions to your challenges. As you continue to read the book, obvious and non-obvious superior solutions can develop.

Exercise 1: Time Shifts

- ❑ Keep my eyes on the prize—"What are we really after?"
- ❑ Sense the significance —"When is the right time to deal with this issue?"
- ❑ Intentionally manage momentum—"What's next?"
- ❑ Keep eyes and ears open to possibilities—"What's on the near and far horizons?"
- ❑ Anticipate patterns —"What's likely to happen?"
- ❑ Congruently act as if there is no time like the present to create the future.

Exercise 2: Interaction Shifts

- ❑ Am I taking action when I shouldn't be—pushing instead of listening?
- ❑ Am I not taking action when I should—dodging instead of informing?
- ❑ Am I being reactive, acting defensively, doing more of the same but thinking I'm doing something different?
- ❑ Am I thinking strategically when I should be tactical, or vice versa?
- ❑ Am I asking, "Do you see it differently?" with my collaborators.
- ❑ Cultivating command presence instead of blaming outside factors.

Exercise 3: Perception Shifts

- ❑ Am I looking at reality or an assumption?
- ❑ Am I stuck in a rule that we are all acting on but not noticing (accepting the givens), instead of creating new rules?
- ❑ Am I worrying instead of asking "How can I do the most with the hand dealt me?"
- ❑ Am I unwittingly committed to consistency—throwing good money after bad?
- ❑ Am I acting with an expert "I know it" attitude instead of an experimental "Let's try it" attitude?
- ❑ Am I willing to listen to objective outside input to shift the possibilities, or do I have a "Do Not Disturb" sign on my mental outlook?

Exercise 4: Structural Shifts

- ❑ Are conflicting goals neutralizing our best efforts?
- ❑ Are we rewarding individual initiative while expecting teamwork?
- ❑ Are we blaming the people rather than seeing the structural forces driving people's behavior?
- ❑ Are we reactively playing to avoid losing rather than proactively playing to win?
- ❑ Are we "doing the strategic math" and generating options or just following the usual path?
- ❑ Determine the strategic hierarchy of what's most important to make the hard decision.

Making strategic shifts can literally move the odds in your favor. Why don't we always make these moves? If you are having trouble finding adequate strategic shifts, you might be up against a hidden timing, interaction, perception, or structural factor. In the next chapter, we look at the obstacles, the Laws of Defeat, that can prevent you from reaching a commanding vantage point.

Steps to Take: Tips and Tools for Shifting

Time Shifts

1. Architect the future: There is no time like the present to create the future.
2. Be a momentum player: Orchestrate rapid forward movement.
3. Use time strategically: Future thinking can change the present action.
4. Anticipate and resolve issues early: Target the developing patterns, the usual and unexpected.

Interaction Shifts

1. Leverage interactions: See the interaction, not the isolated action.
2. Stretch your adaptability rapidly: The person with the widest ranges of responses wins.
3. Collaborate to design simplicity into solutions: Experiment, fail, learn from others, rebound, and simplify.
4. Cultivate command presence: Clarity of mind and the heart of a lion in the face of adversity.

Perception Shifts

1. Proactively approach situations: Play to win rather than to avoid losing.
2. Differentiate hierarchical importance: Know what really matters versus the little stuff.
3. Use dissatisfaction constructively: Spot the weakness and turn it into an advantage.
4. Influence perception: Frame the argument.

Structural Shifts

1. Position to win: Design advantage-making strategies by emphasizing market and customer drivers.
2. Align the structure to produce outcomes: Change the structure, change the behavior.
3. Make the hard decisions: Use your power judiciously; people expect it.
4. Use strategic math: Anticipate the possible outcomes, and design options.

The Advantage-Maker's Advice

Confidence comes to those who perceive reality accurately.
Make it your business to see what there is to see, not what others want you to see.
There is no time like the present to create the future.

Chapter Recap

1. Advantage-making is consistently creating superior outcomes in a timely manner by leveraging assets in the face of constraints, and doing so simply and directly.
2. Constraints are a fact of business life and the opposite of leverage. Advantage-Makers look at constraints as part of the advantage-making materials; they engage the constraint, consciously or otherwise, by putting it to the best possible use.
3. Advantage-Makers strategically shift time, interactions, perceptions, and structures.
4. Timing is the fundamental sense for Advantage-Makers.
5. Interactions determine the relationships between business, organizations, teams, and people.
6. Perception separates the winners from the losers. Winners see options, whereas losers complain.
7. Structure shapes behavior.
8. Shifting time generates possibilities. Shifting perception creates winners. Shifting interactions transforms the game. Shifting structure changes behavior.
9. The Code of the Advantage-Maker enables you to spot opportunities, create advantages, and influence outcomes.

Endnotes

1. Barry X. Lynn, CIO of Wells Fargo, described his strategy during a leadership consulting engagement.

2. Humberto R. Maturana and Francisco J. Varela, *The Tree of Life: The Biological Roots of Human Understanding* (Boston: New Science Library, 1987).

3. Robert Fritz, *Corporate Tides* (San Francisco: Berrett-Koehler, 1996); Leonard Burrello, Lauren Hoffman, and Lynn Murray, *School Leaders Building Capacity from Within: Resolving Competing Agendas Creatively* (Thousand Oaks, CA: Corwin Press, 2004).

4. Richard Bandler and John Grinder, *The Structure of Magic I and II* (Palo Alto, CA: Science & Behavior Books, 1975).

5. Paul Watzlawick, John Weakland, and Richard Fisch, *Change: Principles of Problem Formation and Problem Resolution* (New York, N.Y.: Norton, 1974).

6. J. Hunt, T. Domzai, and J. Kernan, "Causal Attribution and Persuasion: The Case of Disconfirmed Expectancies," in A. Mitchell (ed.) vol. 9, *Advances in Consumer Research* (Ann Arbor, MI: Association for Consumer Research, 1981); R. Settle and L. Gordon, "Attribution Theory and Advertiser Credibility," *Journal of Marketing Research* 11 (1974): 181–185.

7. Pierre Mourier and Martin Smith, *Conquering Organizational Change: How to Succeed where Most Companies Fail* (New York, N.Y.: CEP Press, 2001); B. J. Bashein, M. Lynne Markus, and Patricia Riley, "Business Process Reengineering: Preconditions for Success and How to Prevent Failures," *Information Systems Management*, spring (1994).

8. This Walt Disney story was recounted during a leadership conference.

9. Jan Carlson, *Moments of Truth* (Cambridge, MA: Ballinger, 1987).

10. Richard Schulze, founder and chairman of Best Buy, in "The School of Hard Knocks: What Two Empire Builders Wish They Had Learned in the Classroom," by Patricia B. Gray, *Fortune Small Business Magazine*, 1 March 2006.

11. General Electric CEO Jeff Immelt, in an interview with P&G and GE CEOs Lafley and Immelt, Fortune: C-Suite Strategies Dec. 11, 2006, http://money.cnn.com/magazines/fortune/

12. John Chambers, CEO of Cisco, keynote speech at Stanford Technology Industry Conference, Stanford University, Palo Alto, CA, April 2004.

13. The Wharton Management School gave Dr. Alejandro Zaffaroni the Franklin Institute's Bower Award on April 29, 2005.

14. Richard Branson, Chairman of The Virgin Group, www.virgin.com/AboutVirgin/RichardBranson

15. Jack Welch and Peter Slater, *Get Better or Get Beaten: 31 Leadership Secrets from GE's Jack Welch* (New York, N.Y.: Irwin, 1994).

16. Fast Company.com, "No Satisfaction at Toyota," December 2006, www.fastcompany.com/magazine/111/open_no-satisfaction.html.

17. George Silverman of Market Navigation discussing Apple computers in a personal conversation.

18. Proctor & Gamble CEO A. G. Lafley, in an interview with P&G and GE CEOs Lafley and Immelt, Fortune: C-Suite Strategies Dec. 11, 2006, money.cnn.com/magazines/fortune/fortune_archive/2006/12/11/8395440/index.htm

19. Arthur Blank and Bernard Marcus, "Entrepreneurial Success Stories," in The Public Forum Institute, National Dialogue on Entrepreneurship, www.publicforuminstitute.org/nde/entre/stories/arthur_blank.htm

CHAPTER 3

Wise or Otherwise: Are You Following Any of the Hidden Laws of Defeat?

Men occasionally stumble over the truth, but most of them pick themselves up and hurry off as if nothing happened.

—Winston Churchill

We want our leaders to have penetrating insight and sound judgment, guard against the designs of our competitors, and turn everything to the best possible advantage. Doing so requires commanding vantage points, to get to the eighth floor and see what will create forward movement.

Although we expect our leaders to be wise, they are at times, unfortunately, otherwise. Even smart leaders fall prey to pitfalls that prevent them from reaching the eighth floor—and, worse, they produce disadvantages and need to play cleanup and catch-up.

A leader's judgment develops in the midst of uncertainty. Impaired decisions are not primarily due to bad luck, but timing missteps, interaction errors, perception biases, and structural conflicts.

To improve their sagacity, leaders must avoid what I refer to as the Laws of Defeat. Many studies examine mistakes; this chapter illustrates the surprising mistakes that keep leaders from reaching the eighth floor and achieving a commanding vantage point.

The five Laws of Defeat:

1. Opportunity knocking—do not disturb
2. Perceptual bias—we think we are thinking, but are we?
3. Competing against yourself—at cross purposes
4. Stuck in your persistence—making sticky problems stickier
5. Reactive tendency—playing to avoid losing

Knowing what to avoid might be as important as picking the right target in the first place. At the root of these mistakes is a timing, interaction, perception, or structural error. Each has a remedy that requires you to shift to a different vantage point. Later chapters describe these remedies in the "Tips and Tools" sidebars.

Let's take a look at the five Laws of Defeat and their consequences.

1. Opportunity Knocking—Do Not Disturb

Has opportunity ever knocked on your door and you had a "Do Not Disturb" sign on it?[1] What's worse is that many of us are wearing "Do Not Disturb" signs and we don't realize it. Institutions sometimes have "Do Not Disturb" signs on. For example, does your organization have suggestion boxes that are actually used?

Home Depot was created by several executives who had been fired in a corporate raid. They were dismissed along with their ideas. In the early 1980s, Sears purportedly was considering purchasing Home Depot, but it passed on the deal. Apparently they were looking at their own financial woes and not at the Home Depot proposal. They might have been so focused on making their financial numbers that they couldn't see straight. Big opportunity lost. In the meantime, opportunity kept knocking, and Home Depot built its business powerhouse.[2]

We tend to miss opportunities because we don't *comprehend the strategic context in which we can see a way to win.* Identifying the strategic context before you take action is critical. Miss the strategic context in a meeting with influential people, and you look uninformed, at best, and a fool to less compassionate colleagues. Your competency is revealed in your ability to get the lay of the land quickly and accurately, to get the big picture and the relevant details—both make a difference.

Trap: Narrow Thinking

The challenge is opportunity myopia—when narrow thinking rules your behavior. Contrary to popular leadership gospel, managers can miss the strategic context and real opportunities when they're stuck in their "stay focused only" mentality.

We continuously hear people implore us to focus. Yet that very common refrain, "Focus," might result in overlooking an opportunity that sits in front of us. Sometimes we are simply focusing on the wrong thing. Of course, focusing is important, yet imposing a focus can blur judgment on when to fold a losing hand.

People tend to become too narrow when attempting to size up a situation. Management guru Peter Drucker says the critical factor in effective management is listening before you speak.[3] That is a good general idea, but what should you listen for? I believe you should listen for the strategic context. If you are listening for what you already know, you won't see what you don't know.

The most surprising factor that causes people to miss the strategic context is the goal error. Management by objectives is useful but can become problematic. When goals and objectives have a predetermined character, they tend to delete or distort any possibility that doesn't fit into them. Imposed goals discourage questioning what you are doing and can do. As such, you don't see opportunities that are available.

Although keeping your eye on the prize is essential, keeping your eye on the strategic context includes both the desired outcome and the environment in which action takes place.

Imposed negotiation deadlines have a similar effect: They narrow the focus and miss options. For most managers, being out of focus seems like a bad thing—and it can be. A mistake managers make in strategy sessions is being company-centric rather than customer-centric. This results in good ideas that the customer doesn't want.

Jack Trout asserts that goal setting is the downfall of good marketing programs.[4] Executives miss the unexpected opportunities. An unquestioned standard can lead to excessive dependence on one product. Markets that could have been capitalized on are missed. The question to ask is, "Is this standard or convention causing us to miss an opportunity?" Making a profit is a good thing; however, if profit objectives dominate at the cost of seeing opportunities, the profit objective is counterproductive, as illustrated in the Home Depot case.

Blindsided by Our Blind Spots

Our ability to see from the eighth floor is reduced by blind spots that go undetected. We are, in effect, blindsided by our blind spots. One particularly pernicious blind spot is making things more complex than they need to be. People confuse complexity with difficulty. Detail complexity can overwhelm decision makers and often results in not making hard choices. Advantages cannot be developed because we are looking at the details rather than the patterns that reveal opportunities.

Opportunity Is Knocking, But No One Is Home

It's easier for outsiders to bring innovations to the table than it is for those who work there. Home Depot's founders had to leave their old company to be successful.

Advantage-Makers encounter the "Do Not Disturb" sign wherever they meet short-sightedness. They are the Galileos of the twenty-first century. It's not that every idea is a good idea and should be funded; the problem here is a more pernicious tendency. People don't even realize they are doing it.

The justification list is long, but these are a few common "Do Not Disturb" responses:

- No time.
- We don't do that kind of ....
- I'm overwhelmed as it is.
- We are cutting costs.
- If it wasn't invented here, we are not interested.
- We tried that before (without noticing the fundamental differences).
- Okay, tell me your idea (but I have preset category killers).

Imagine doing this to your children, giving them a "Do Not Disturb" response when they are developing their interests:

"Dad, I have this idea."

"Sorry, son, but I don't have time."

"Sorry, sweetie, but we don't have the energy to listen to your life's ambition to save the world."

As often as we inadvertently dismiss children, we can dismiss opportunities as well.

Would you have recognized the opportunity that Levi Strauss did in 1849? During the California Gold Rush, he traveled to San Francisco with bolts of cloth to manufacture tents for the miners. It seemed like a good idea at the time, but Strauss found that miners had something else on their minds. The miners wanted pants that could withstand the rugged mining activities. He didn't say, "Sorry, I'm in the tent business." He began Levi-Strauss blue jeans and lined his pockets with gold.

If You Don't See the Patterns, You Won't See the Opportunities

Silos in organizations and in thinking result in missed strategic contexts. An executive almost lost his job because he couldn't see outside his own domain. He paid attention to his department to the exclusion of the rest of the company. Besides being politically dense, he didn't see the relationship between his group and key functions within the organization. Why did the executive make that mistake? On the face of it, this problem seems so ridiculous that it almost calls into question the executive's ability. Yet when you are caught in single-point focusing, you lose your objectivity. This executive kept trying to force-fit the people and task into a preconceived way of operating. It seldom works.

In contrast, when military generals create a strategy, they take a broad view of the situation, and they see the network of connections they will encounter. They find a strategic vantage point to inform their judgment.

Our judgment is affected by the scope of our focus. The narrower our scope, the more likely we will overlook relevant data. Advantage-Makers shift to the strategic context and attend to a network of possibilities. Take off the opportunity blinders.

2. Perceptual Bias and Error— We Think We Are Thinking, but Are We?

The notion that "perception is reality" is popular. Human beings are, in fact, perceivers. We are perceivers of a real world. Whether we perceive the real world correctly is open to dialogue and, unfortunately, conflict. One of the easiest mistakes leaders fall prey to is confusing perception with reality. We don't see that we don't see. The blinds are down on the windows of the eighth floor. As a consequence, we don't confront reality as effectively. Leaders who don't have a good fix on the reality they are up against will be hampered in their search for advantages.

The following is a set of well-known perceptual biases and errors that undermine and cloud the lenses of Advantage-Makers. This is not an exhaustive list; it targets specific traps to advantage-making.

Availability Bias

Research has confirmed the tendency for people to base their judgments on information that is readily available to them.[5] In other words, if you are writing a performance appraisal of a subordinate, you will think of the information that is either the most recent or the most emotionally vivid in your mind. This might explain why subordinates say that once their bosses form a strong opinion of them, it is hard to change their minds.

As long as the employees began with good marks or weren't too bad early on, they might use this bias to their advantage—focusing their work efforts just a few months before the appraisals.

Are people really thinking and seeing what there is to see, or are they simply processing the most available memories?

Representative Bias

This is the automatic tendency to compare something with what you already know, even when it is not an appropriate analogy.[6] For example, a manager could compare a new product with an existing product in terms of potential for success. This could be dead wrong. This bias is also seen in the unexamined assumption that if you come from the same school as a new hire, you think he or she will perform in similar ways to you. The representative bias reduces your advantage-making to what you already know, thus letting you see only what you know to see. Spotting opportunities with this biased lens is particularly hard. What's worse is that you won't realize you are in jeopardy unless you spotlight the bias and look for differences.

Unchecked Consistency Error—Too Much of a Good Thing

We want to be consistent and appear consistent. We value consistency in our working relations. Leon Festinger has amply demonstrated that consistency is a central motivator of behavior.[7] It is a powerful social influence. We view inconsistent people as unreliable. Managers who are hit-or-miss producers are held in low regard. In sports, we lose confidence in players who are inconsistent. Consistency is highly valued.

Robert Cialdini reports that the heuristic, or rule of thumb, is to act consistent with what we have successfully done before.[8] Yet our success from the past might actually prevent us from seeing the reality and opportunity of the present. Unchecked consistency squelches innovations and invention. In fact, it cost a manufacturing company millions of dollars. The CEO's tendency for consistency, tied to his desire to maintain order, was imposed upon his strategic decisions. He rejected a viable business option, and, instead of changing what wasn't working, he insisted on staying the course. Looking back, he realized that his insistence on order had overlooked an opportunity. Order was more important than opportunity. He is not alone in this error: We jump to conclusions based upon the need to be consistent.

The Trap: The Commitment Error

According to Cialdini, social psychologists have found that the key ingredient in fostering consistency is commitment.[9] When we make a commitment, we try to be consistent with it. A small, seemingly harmless statement commits us to a course of action, and instead of changing, we keep investing—counterproductively. Advantage-Makers cannot afford to allow consistency to dictate their strategic shifting.

We are committed to our way of doing things, especially if we say so publicly. It is easier to not think, to just go along with our past view. We become dogmatic rather than considering the pros and cons. Our consistency is like a foot in the door that, once set, won't leave until we reaffirm our commitment to the way we have done it before.

Acting consistent is generally a good navigational tool, but a faulty setting is problematic. A biotech CEO was worried about his conclusion-jumping vice president. Based upon what the vice president already believed, he continued to make decisions without discriminating between issues, resulting in significant losses.

Unquestioned consistency can lead to defeat. We don't check the current reality of our assumptions. It can be a rut that keeps us stuck. We shoot the messenger of bad news. In tragic cases, our egocentrism results in "captainitis"—when an airline pilot ignores the input from his crew and flies the plane into harm's way with deadly results.[10]

In business, when you have made a conclusion in the past about how things work, you try to stick with it. This valued strength—consistency, commitment to your word, and dependability—can make it extremely difficult to question underlying assumptions. We don't want to see ourselves—or have others see us—as inconsistent. For this reason, unchecked consistency squelches innovations and invention.

Anchor Bias

What's your reference point on any issue you are dealing with? Few, if any, of us recognize the power of the reference point. It anchors us to a point of view. It prevents us from getting to a commanding vantage point. It wears disguises, as if it were the only place from which to see the issue, and we fall for the ruse.

Your perception is altered by the reference point your ideas are framed against. When baselines are established, they shape your thinking. Scott Plous wondered whether independent thinkers can be unwittingly influenced by worst-case or best-case scenarios.[11] Do you think that you, as an independent thinker, can be influenced simply by shifting your attention to extremes? Want examples? Just answer polling questions or listen to how the news is reported.

Much to our chagrin, Amos Tversky and Daniel Kahneman have consistently verified our tendency to fixate on initial information.[12] If your task is to influence someone, the reference point you establish will support or undermine your objective. People will relate to you differently if they think of you as a turnaround specialist or a leader who grows companies. Choose your anchors wisely, or they will weigh you down. As a decision maker and influencer, these results are of paramount importance to your effectiveness.

In the marketplace, we are exposed to this anchoring effect on a daily basis. The leading brands own the position in our minds and markets, and they are hard to dislodge.

In negotiations, we are anchored to the initial offer—quickly. You hardly notice the anchor—the asking price of your home, or the price of your service. Yet it establishes the context and shapes your decision.

Adjustments Are Inadequate

Tversky and Kahneman identified a critical aspect of this bias: People don't make an appropriate adjustment, up or down, from the anchor.[13] First impressions count more. Anchors are powerful factors of influence that become even more significant during times of uncertainty. The tendency is to fixate on initial conditions and information—the givens. *We take the givens as gospel.* Our ability to spot opportunities is reduced by this tendency. When we have that starting point, it is difficult to adjust—we get anchored to initial information. As we receive new information, it has a hard time registering because the starting information has more weight in our minds.

Overconfidence Bias

Two months before the disastrous Chernobyl nuclear plant meltdown, the Minister of Power and Electrification in the Ukraine said, "The odds of a meltdown are one in 10,000 years!"

Advantage-Makers are not shrinking violets, but they do not get trapped into thinking they know more than they do. Overconfidence keeps you from getting to a commanding vantage point, because you can't see potential danger and countermoves.

Overconfidence is a real threat to a leader's efficacy. Research by Sarah Lichtenstein and Baruch Fischhoff found that when people were 70% confident of being right, they were, in fact, correct 50% of the time.[14] The gap between accuracy and confidence in their estimates is significant.

People who are weakest in interpersonal skills tend to overestimate their performance ability. This is a real conundrum for leaders who are building teams. Humility is essential; without it, the overconfidence bias can undermine an Advantage-Maker's thought process. Have you ever been 100% sure, yet dead wrong?

Fischhoff and Slovic, et al., found the overconfidence bias even more problematic; people who thought they were 100% sure of their decision were, in fact, wrong 15%–30% of the time.[15]

The Trap: Overestimating and Underestimating

Overconfidence is activated by either overestimating ability or underestimating the challenge. During an organizational change, a high-tech manager requested a more senior role. The executive denied the request, and the direct report was quite upset. The role required someone with the right competencies upon assuming the position. This manager simply didn't have those abilities right now. The direct report felt he had grown professionally and was ready for a bigger job. The executive agreed that the manager had grown, but not sufficiently to fulfill the role immediately. It was a high-stakes role, and the person just wasn't ready.

This is a classic case of someone overestimating what he or she had demonstrated and underestimating the requirements. Although it was true that the individual had grown, it was equally true that the position required an experienced senior performer immediately. There wasn't time to learn on the job. Individuals make the mistake of evaluating themselves based upon where they have come from, rather than where they need to be. The standard of measurement is confused, looking at the starting line rather than the finish line. As a consequence, the direct report's certainty was actually inappropriate.

What's the consequence of people under-or-over-estimating? They miss the reality and thus misjudge the situation. They can't distinguish between what matters and what is just noise, between the things that will make a difference and doing a lot of busywork. This becomes particularly problematic when they miss it by an order of magnitude that is disturbing to the parties involved.

Let's look a little more closely at the role change example first presented. If you are rated a 4 on performance and the next time around you rate a 7, that might seem terrific. You've improved 75%. How many people can clearly state that unambiguously? These appear to be impressive results, but perhaps not sufficient for the task at hand. If the measure is based upon where you started, this grade is beyond satisfactory. If the measure is based upon where you need to be—let's say 10—you have fallen short and the result will be seen as inadequate, no matter what progress has been made.

Consider the situation with the CEO who tells one of the members of her executive staff that he needs to improve his performance by "an order of magnitude." That's a big deal. When the VP is asked about the seriousness of the issues, he states that just a few areas are in need of improvement, but overall performance is fine and that fixing these areas will help the storm pass quickly. Obviously, a discrepancy exists between their understandings.

Managers typically underestimate the level of change needed to achieve the performance improvements. How can we explain this? When people estimate the change others need to do, it's quite high; but when they estimate the change they need to do, it's lower.

Obviously people actually are able to accurately see what needs to be done. The point here is that over-or-under estimation can chip away at the advantage-making capacity.

Individuals tend to overweight the information they deem relevant while underweighting the rest of the information.[16] What is striking about this is that people pay attention to only a small portion of the available and relevant information. This kind of mistake actually leads us to look at one final error—the fundamental attribution error.

Fundamental Attribution Error[17]

When making judgments, we tend to over-attribute personal factors and under-attribute situational forces. People default to the individual as cause, instead of the situation as cause. The consequence is erroneous explanations for behavior. The problem occurs predominantly because of the lack of a vantage point to see what is really happening.

For example, imagine that a sales manager is let go because he hasn't made his quota. We know the sales manager, we see his behavior, we hear his complaints—our focus is on him. We might underestimate or not see the competitor's stronger product line. Psychologically, our attention goes to what is most "salient" to us.

This bias extends to attributing our successes to ourselves, and our failures to the situation. A manager who receives critical feedback might minimize the message. When we have a weakness, the fundamental attribution error might diminish our failings or elevate our know-how. At a minimum, the fundamental attribution error distorts critical feedback. Within the organization this is commonly known as the "they don't get it" phenomenon. These tendencies can undermine any ability for an Advantage-Maker to correct course. (Recall that "reading situations" and rapidly course-correcting are key skills of Advantage-Makers.)

3. Competing against Yourself—At Cross Purposes

Competition has contributed to advancing civilization, as has cooperation. Competition in the marketplace is expected to provide consumers with better products at lower prices. At a minimum, competition drives efficiencies.

Businesses compete—that's a given. You want to win. You want to defend yourself in the marketplace. When you place challenges in front of yourself, to be better than you have been, this tends to create momentum in the right direction. Competition of ideas pushes and challenges people to rigorous inquiry and achieving higher levels.

Businesses are, however, shooting themselves in the foot by competing against themselves. Many companies want to do more with less—to run lean. Yet when they are at cross purposes with themselves, they do less with more. Let's take a quick look at how companies can actually paint themselves into a disadvantage by competing against themselves:

- You are competing against yourself when you've determined that a team-based organizational design would be most productive while you accentuate, reward, and incentivize individual performance goals that are in conflict with the team. The consequence is you have employee infighting, dysfunctional behavior, morale problems, and bad-mouthing of others. Change the reward structure and the behavior will shift.

- You are competing against yourself when you tell people to push for growth while simultaneously pushing for cost savings in the wrong places. As a consequence, you weaken both objectives.

- You are competing against yourself when people in the organization are given a mandate but are not given adequate decision-making authority to carry it out. The consequence is delay, conflict, ineffective performance, increased head count, and misused resources. Grant the appropriate decision-making authority.

- You are competing against yourself when you place the culture above the business strategy. The consequence is a loss of focus on the business objectives. Levi-Strauss made this error—it lost billions of dollars of capitalization. This doesn't minimize culture; instead, it recommends positioning the culture to support the business strategy, rather than vice versa.

- You are competing against yourself when you have the same engineers tasked to maintain the existing product line while at the same time scheduling them for new releases. They might not be able to adequately allocate their efforts and might end up being blamed for missing targets on both objectives. Determine what percentage of their time they should allocate to each, or decide what is most important.

- You are competing against yourself when you promote innovation but punish mistakes. The consequences are fewer mistakes and fewer innovations.

- You are competing against yourself if you are committed to total quality yet reward only shipping on schedule—even with defects—and punish people if it doesn't go out. This produces lack of alignment. It is not a psychological issue or a people issue; it is a structural issue. Change the structure, and the behavior will change.

Competing against yourself is more than the right hand not knowing what the left hand is doing. The right hand is fighting with the left hand, even if inadvertently. An insidious way you are competing against yourself is when you argue about the importance of confronting reality but allow people to deflect from the real issues.

On average, 65% of change efforts fail.[18] Why? Because the underlying performance structure is competing against the change.[19] Ever been on a waterslide? How much control do you have? Not much. The slide is an underlying structure that determines the behavior as you move. Similarly, you have an underlying structure that drives behavior in your organization. Change the waterslide, and people will move differently. This topic is the focus of Chapter 7, "Move or Lose: Manage Momentum to Advance Your Organization."

4. Stuck in Persistence— Making Sticky Problems Stickier

If at first you don't succeed, try, try again. Persistence is a virtue. Determination is vital to success. All of these are true. Yet what happens when you get stuck in your persistence? Have you ever considered that your attempted solutions keep fueling the fire? That's true in the interpersonal realm, but what about in the organizational realm, when you persist with projects that are not working? Throw more resources at them. That's the tendency, isn't it? Yet the more you continue the same approach, the more you get stuck in persisting with decisions that offer little, if any, reward. Your persistence at an interpersonal level—or, for that matter, in any business situation—can make a sticky problem stickier.

We can use the Avis example to point to the repetitive hopes of beating Hertz by doing more of the same—just keep on keeping on. How many strategic initiatives do you keep investing in past their expiration date?

As I was discussing this specific Law of Defeat during a strategic offsite meeting, CEO Jim Bailey realized that his company had projects that needed to be reviewed with a critical eye toward "stuck on persistence." It was time to turn off the faucet.

It's particularly difficult to do this for a number of reasons, the biggest of which is the virtue of persistence in the face of adversity. Re-investing resources in failing ventures is a tough call, yet continuing to do more of the same places you at a further disadvantage.

The challenge is actually worse than overcoming the virtue of persistence. Often the attempted solutions you believe will fix things are contributing to the problem. You're weakened by your strengths and can't see that repeating this behavior or decision will only maintain the status quo problem. For example, the more you, as the boss, tell people what to do on all projects, the more your employees don't develop their own ideas and skills; the more they don't develop their own ideas and skills, the less you think they are capable of doing the job without your input. And on you persist with well-intentioned behavior, hardly to anyone's advantage.

Your persistence is misguided but well intended. Know any roads like that? Chapter 6, "The Game Changer: If You Are in a Hole, Stop Digging and Change the Game," is devoted to solutions when getting "stuck in persistence."

Not wanting to deal with conflict, executives let problems fester and fall prey to reactive organizations.

5. Reactive—Playing to Avoid Losing

You can be defeated by your reactive tendencies. A fundamental difference exists between reacting against difficulties and creating outcomes in the face of difficulties. When you are outcome-oriented, your emphasis is on achieving the outcome; you play to win rather than complaining or blaming the circumstances. Reactive mishandling of situations almost always guarantees lower outcomes. Others might trigger us to react to their challenges; they blame us for their condition. We might act as if we are victims of circumstances when we aren't.

Recently, at a restaurant, our harried waitress was behind and trying to catch up. At first, we waited patiently, but as our hunger grew, so did our impatience. Finally, she arrived at our table, and without missing a beat, she explained, "You are a victim of my circumstances!" Although this is a humorous interaction and a momentary distraction, people acting powerless often blame others and/or their circumstances.

Professionally competent CEOs can get caught in a vicious reactive cycle. An executive wanted to increase his company's business from $80 million to $200 million in five years. He worked hard at creating a strategy but was discouraged with the slow progress. Yet when anyone proposed well-thought-out and researched expansion plans, such as adding a new product line or reinventing an old market, he would resist.

If you asked the executive what he did all day, he would say he worked hard on the growth of his company. Finally he stopped to examine what was going wrong with his approach. He realized his mind-set was to avoid risk, which was not consistent with his company's commitment to real growth. He was reacting against his fear, allowing it to determine his course of action. What he was doing wasn't working. Reactivity is one of the major derailers in the executive suite—we become defensive when things don't go our way.

Mishandling situations can set you back. Reactive behavior often has a sense of powerlessness at its root. As an Advantage-Maker, your choice is to move forward and use the momentum to keep advancing.

Reactive organizations are usually in crisis mode. We see short-term fixes to get rid of the immediate problem. The downside is burnout and poor decision-making tendencies. Let's be clear: Real crises exist, and they must be dealt with immediately.

Hurricane Katrina in New Orleans was a real crisis that wasn't responded to effectively, with catastrophic consequences. A real crisis shouldn't be confused with a reactive pattern that, in itself, leads to more crises and a never-ending cycle. Combining constraints with reactive tendencies reduces your advantage-making capacity.

Take this test to see if you are being reactive:

Reactive Trap Test

- ❑ Are you playing to avoid losing?
- ❑ Are you acting defensive when there is no need to defend yourself?
- ❑ Are you letting the circumstance determine your actions?
- ❑ Are you trying to control things you can't or don't control?
- ❑ Are you acting obligated to things you haven't agreed to?
- ❑ Are you acting powerless, as if things won't work out when you handle difficulties?
- ❑ Are you tending to complain about problems rather than creating outcomes?

Detection Is Key

Each of these five errors can turn into your defeat. The Laws of Defeat prevent you from spotting opportunities, creating advantages, and influencing outcomes. By making them the boundaries that you pay attention to and course-correct from, you increase your odds of succeeding.

Avoiding these Laws of Defeat helps establish a clearer vantage point. Shifting away from these biases and errors improves your results; paradoxically, it fosters strategic ingenuity. Knowing about these errors enables you to self-regulate, skillfully adapt to rapid changes, and snatch victory from the Laws of Defeat.

Steps to Take

1. Become familiar with these five Laws of Defeat.
2. Notice every day how you and your colleagues violate these Laws of Defeat.
3. Select one Law of Defeat and focus on reducing it in your daily actions. For example, notice how the anchoring bias affects your decisions. If you are weighed down by an anchor, exaggerate the opposite. When you are limited to $55,000 in a negotiation, imagine that you could be offered $200,000. Then consider what you would do differently. Is this still a good deal?
4. Use the reactive tendency test and spot the times when you are reacting. If you are blaming or complaining, take a brief time-out. Then think, "What am I trying to create here? What outcome do I want to achieve?" This should shift you into a more proactive stance and get you moving in the right direction.
5. When you are told that you need to improve your performance, consider if you are underestimating what is actually required. Then consider making more change than discussed.
6. When you are focusing on a project, pause long enough to consider the strategic context in which you are acting. Keep an eye out for opportunities as you ward off the "Do Not Disturb" sign that wants to find its way onto you.
7. Are you stuck in persistence—for example, are you throwing good money after bad? If a project isn't working, consider what an outsider who just took over the decision would do. Would they keep investing in the project? Request brutally honest feedback from other Advantage-Makers.

The Advantage-Maker's Advice

Steer toward opportunity and away from defeat.
Let's call those things you should avoid "noxiants."[20]
The Laws of Defeat are noxiants to shift you into rapid course correction.
This guidance system enables you to question faulty assumptions.
A shift in the guidance system steers you to new opportunity.

Chapter Recap

Detect these five Laws of Defeat early:

Opportunity Knocking: Do Not Disturb

- Avoid the imposition of goals.
- Avoid missing the strategic context.
- Avoid the inadvertent "Do Not Disturb" error.
- Avoid making things unnecessarily complex.

Perceptual Bias and Error: We Think We Are Thinking, but Are We?

- Avoid the availability bias.
- Avoid the familiar representation bias.
- Avoid unchecked commitment to consistency.
- Avoid the anchor error.
- Avoid overconfidence by under-and-over estimating.
- Avoid the fundamental attribution error.

Competing Against Yourself: At Cross Purposes

- Avoid inadvertently fighting against yourself.
- Avoid competing goals.
- Avoid inadequate decision authority.

Stuck on Persistence: Making Sticky Problems Stickier

- Avoid doing more of the same, harder.
- Avoid throwing good money after bad.

Reactive Tendencies: Playing to Avoid Losing

- Avoid complaining rather than solving.
- Avoid defensive behavior.

Endnotes

1. Roger Von Oech, *A Whack on the Side of the Head* (New York, N.Y.: Warner Books, 1983).

2. Arthur Blank and Bernard Marcus, Entrepreneurial Success Stories, in The Public Forum Institute, National Dialogue on Entrepreneurship, www.publicforuminstitute.org/nde/entre/stories/arthur_blank.htm.

3. Peter Drucker, *The Essential Drucker* (New York, N.Y.: HarperCollins, 2005).

4. Jack Trout, *Trout on Strategy* (New York: McGraw-Hill, 2004).

5. Amos Tversky and Daniel Kahneman, "Judgment Under Uncertainty: Heuristics and Biases," *Science* 185 (1974), 1124–1130.

6. *Ibid.*

7. Leon Festinger, *The Theory of Cognitive Dissonance* (New York: Harper and Row, 1957).

8. Robert Cialdini, *Influence: Science and Practice,* 4th ed. (Cambridge, MA: Allyn & Bacon, 2001).

9. *Ibid.*

10. H. Clayton Foushee, "Dyads and Triads at 35,000 Feet: Factors Affecting Group Process and Aircraft Performance," *American Psychologist* 39 (1984), 885–893.

11. Scott Plous, *The Psychology of Judgment and Decision Making* (New York, N.Y.: McGraw-Hill, 1993).

12. Amos Tversky and Daniel Kahneman, "Judgment Under Uncertainty: Heuristics and Biases," *Science*, 211, 453–458, 1974.

13. *Ibid.*

14. Sarah Lichtenstein and Baruch Fischhoff, "Do those who know more also know more about how much they know?" *Organizational Behavior and Human Performance*, 26, 1977, 149–171.

15. Baruch Fischhoff, Paul Slovic, and Sarah Lichtenstein, "Knowing with certainty: The appropriateness of extreme confidence," *Journal of Experimental Psychology*, Human Perception and Performance, 1977, 3, 253–285.

16. Kahneman and Tversky, *Choices, Values and Frames*: Cambridge University Press, (New York, N.Y.: Cambridge University Press, 2000).

17. Lee Ross, "The Intuitive Psychologist and His Shortcomings: Distortions in the Attribution Process," in L. Berkowitz (ed.), vol. 10, *Advances in Experimental Social Psychology* (New York: Academic Press, 1977).

18. Pierre Mourier and Martin Smith, *Conquering Organizational Change: How to Succeed Where Most Companies Fail* (New York, N.Y.: CEP Press, 2001); B. J. Bashein, M. Lynne Markus, and Patricia Riley, "Business Process Reengineering: Preconditions for Success and How to Prevent Failures," *Information Systems Management*, spring (1994).

19. Robert Fritz, *The Path of Least Resistance for Managers* (San Francisco: Berrett-Koehler, 1999).

20. Gareth Morgan, *Images of the Organization* (Newbury Park, CA: Sage Publications, 1986).

CHAPTER 4

Shifting to a Commanding (Ad)Vantage Point

The key to the future is the ability to think on the edge of one's culture.

—Jennifer James, Ph.D.

Morale problems at a national retailer grabbed the executives' attention. Normally, when problems arise, the tendency is to find a quick solution to fix the complaint. These managers thought a team-building exercise would energize and inspire their people again. It sounded like good, proactive common sense. Was there anything wrong with this? It's a question of vantage points. If team building would move the organization strategically forward, they chose wisely. However, the real issue was not teamwork, as they assumed, but rather an inadequate business strategy. People were arguing because they were confused about the organization's direction. Therefore, no amount of team building would make the real problem disappear. A quick team fix would be temporary. As soon as they got back to the office, they would all return to their old habits and complaints.

Advantage-Makers must answer the question "What's actually driving the behavior?" In this case, what is driving the morale problem? When people aren't getting along, managers typically pick the first "off-the-shelf" solution that seems good enough—team building.

Let's consider what actually happened behind the scenes of the team-building event. Criticism increased because people felt they were being sent to charm school (a.k.a. team building) instead of dealing with the real problem. The leader lost credibility without knowing it. People attended the team-building event without engaging. This continued until someone finally said, "You know, the real problem is not teamwork, but lack of agreement on the business strategy." Time, effort, money, and patience were wasted.

If the executives had looked at what was actually happening, it would have become obvious that the issue was only partially related to teamwork. Most people had good intentions, and those who were complaining about the others in the group were just misplacing the cause of the problem on the people in the group. Examining the situation from the vantage point of the customer and suppliers, a lack of strategic clarity was causing the confusion and conflict. The strategic issue needed to be corrected first. Any team issues related to implementing the strategy change should then be addressed.

Solving the wrong problem is not a new problem. Well-intentioned people do it all the time. However, opportunities are overlooked because of a limited point of view.

Try This Experiment

To shift to a commanding vantage point for the team example, consider this thought experiment:

1. If everyone were well-intentioned but the strategy continued to be unclear, what kind of interactions might you predict?
2. If the strategy were clarified, what would the nature of the team interactions be?

The answer to the first question points to the morale problems and unwanted behavior. The answer to the second question enables you to imagine positive team behavior. If you "do the math" on this situation, it helps you determine the right course of action.

The Principle: Strategic Shifting to a Commanding Vantage Point

Why do you want a vantage point?

It positions you, similar to a strategic hill on a battlefield. A strategic hill serves as a vantage point from which to look at situations and see reality clearly. Moreover, your power to see opportunities in the face of adversity increases, as does grasping your allies' and competitors' objectives. The likelihood of being fooled or misguided is less. Your arguments become more cogent and convincing with your colleagues.

Strategic shifting equips leaders with a set of distinctions—time, interaction, perceptions, and structures—that enables them to see opportunity, create advantages, and influence outcomes. The equipment for strategic shifting consists of four Advantage Points:

1. **Adapt and stretch**—The person with the widest range of responses wins. Mental agility and rapid adaptation expand your maneuverability (see Chapter 5, "Adaptive Stretching: It's Not the Best Who Wins—It's Who's the Most Adaptive").

2. **Change the game**—Instead of persisting with what isn't working, do something unexpected for a change. Show the fly the way out of the bottle (see Chapter 6, "The Game Changer: If You Are in a Hole, Stop Digging and Change the Game").

3. **Move or lose**—Position yourself for forward movement, or your best efforts could be neutralized (see Chapter 7, "Move or Lose: Manage Momentum to Advance Your Organization").

4. **Influence perception**—Small, influential moves can yield big leverage gains. This creates a multiplier effect (see Chapter 8,

"Strategic Influence: How to Get People to Say Yes in the Right Way to the Right Things," and Chapter 9, "Influence Perception: Helping People See What They Need to See").

When adopted, these frameworks shift your perception to commanding vantage points. Leaders are better able to clarify intention, direction, protection and action for their organizations.

Advantage Points reduce your blind spots. You can be blindsided when driving your car unless you turn your head to check in your blind spot area. Real danger exists when you don't recognize your blind spots. When you turn your head, you shift your scope of attention and see things that you overlooked. In similar ways, we can use the four Advantage Points to shift our attention to see things that we overlook.

Stuck in a Formula

When we are stuck in a formula, we fail to see what there is to see. The introduction of New Coke into the marketplace was a marketing disaster. Coca-Cola performed extensive research but missed a dimension that influenced customer decisions. People preferred the taste of New Coke, but it was the wrong measure; Coca-Cola underestimated the dimension of taking a national favorite—traditional Coke—off the shelves. If they'd had the Advantage Point of what influences perception, as discussed in Chapter 8, their research might have revealed a more profitable course of action.

Sometimes conventional wisdom can leave you in a rut while things are changing around you. IBM didn't shift quickly enough with the computer age; they lost millions of dollars and had to play catch-up. Not only can you mishandle difficulties, but conventional wisdom can miss opportunities. Most of us have been sitting in front of a cup of coffee every morning for years. Starbucks smelled the coffee. Now there are thousands of Starbucks—shift, shift, shift.

Shifting to Match the Real Issue

Knowing the appropriate shift to make is critical to success, and Advantage-Makers shift their responses to match the situation. For example, they shift from thinking that they are dealing with a collaboration issue when, in fact, they are facing a product issue, or vice versa.

Managers look at problems in terms of categories—as a systems, process, structural, or people issue. You have your favorite fix. Yet you might overlook a dimension in which you can actually find solutions.

Shifting to Spot Hidden Opportunity

When faced with difficulty, the question that Advantage-Makers must consider is, "Which vantage point will be most advantageous here?" Consider timing, interactions, perception, or structure.

History is replete with examples of those who created opportunity where others didn't see it. People were looking in the wrong places or the wrong dimensions. Although many people can see, they still do not shift.

Dr. Alexander Fleming was engaged in an experiment in his lab. A troublesome mold had killed the bacteria culture he was studying. This was not a good thing, unless you make a dimensional shift in your thought process, as Dr. Fleming did. He no longer saw the mold as a problem, but as a solution to another problem of getting rid of unwanted bacteria—and he discovered penicillin.[1]

Advantage-Makers don't need to have all the answers; they spot either the vantage point or the person who has the better vantage point and can make the right recommendations.

Defining Vantage Points

Vantage points frame your perception. When your vantage point is limited, your perception is limited. Not all vantage points are equal. The most advantageous position might not be the same as your personal feeling, concept, or experience. When things go wrong, you can often trace the problem back to an incorrect vantage point.

Managers substitute their skill set for a vantage point. For example, analytically oriented managers evaluate the right thing to do based upon a causal analysis, and sales managers focus on revenue generation. Neither of these is inherently wrong, but neither is inherently right.

Just as you shouldn't confuse your blind spot or weakness with your strength, you shouldn't confuse your strength with what is necessary. Your talent might be in solving engineering problems, but is that what is needed now? A few years ago, General Motors made a classic error when they allowed the finance people to control, influence, and otherwise design cars based predominantly on financial specifications instead of good car design specifications. Not enough people wanted to buy a car built by a finance mind. The finance people should have done their finance work, letting the designers design the cars. Ironically, GM lost a lot of money with finance's designs.

Vantage points are positions, conditions, situations, or opportunities that provide superiority or advantage. A commanding, comprehensive outlook.

In *Webster's Revised Unabridged Dictionary,* the term *vantage point* is defined as follows:

> A position, condition, situation, or opportunity that is likely to provide superiority or an advantage, especially a comprehensive view or commanding perspective. A superior or more favorable situation or opportunity; gain; profit; advantage.

As you can see, vantage points come in many forms. Any place has a point of view. Any idea has a point of view. However, only a few places and ideas are commanding vantage points that give you a favorable advantage. Wisdom develops from cultivating your vantage points.

Spotting an Advantage Point

Advantage Points are initially spotted by taking the following actions:
1. Identifying the target and sensing if you are going in the right direction
2. Contrasting what is believed to be true to what is really true
3. Comparing the current outcomes to the results you are seeking
4. Shifting from what isn't working to changing the game (see Chapter 6)

When John F. Kennedy set the United States on the path to landing a man on the moon and bringing the crew safely home, his commanding vantage point saw an opportunity to transform America, and propelled us into the Space Age.

By definition, a vantage point differs from an individual opinion or subjective impression. A personal opinion or subjective impression is a perception that may or may not actually reflect reality.

Personal points of view are necessary but insufficient. Every point of view is a perspective. You have your point of view, and I have mine, so let's try to understand each other. That's appropriate and essential in many conversations. However, it is inadequate for leadership or making final judgments. "Getting it right" is the province of leadership. Our opinions matter, but they can be right or wrong without serious effect. Leadership has consequences, and as such, having a commanding vantage point is imperative.

A vantage point is not a mystical place. Because you need to sense whether you are going in the right direction, it can sometimes seem that way. Advantage Points are directional. Without a vantage point, you will not go in the right direction. If your vantage point is obstructed, your power to produce advantage will be skewed, and the organization will be at a disadvantage.

Vantage Points Are Dynamic

Position yourself, behaviorally, at the most opportune place to create advantage. Wayne Gretsky, a hall-of-fame hockey player known as The Great One (also the top scorer, and arguably the greatest hockey player, of all time), was said to be able to read the ice—he could anticipate where the puck was going to be on the ice. Seeing the movement of the game was his vantage point, and he positioned himself to be able to score. His quote "You miss 100% of the shots you never take" illustrates his vantage point. Obviously, he wasn't overly concerned with missing; instead, he wanted to score and have the opportunity to score. His vantage point is a key for getting the most out of everything you have and not squandering opportunities.

On teams, the idea that works is important, not the individual's position. The secretary might have a better vantage point than the manager. Conversely, frontline people might get caught up in the details and miss the big picture. Listen to whoever has the right vantage point. Play to his or her strength. Advantage-Makers set aside their egos to spot opportunity.

Dynamics shifts have generated disruptive technologies, and entrepreneurs outmaneuver mature industries. There are no once and for all times answers, nor should you look for the perfect vantage point. As times shift so do vantage points.

Strategic Shifting Competencies

1. Rapidly position yourself at Advantage Points to spot opportunities.
2. Shift your mental vantage point to different angles of the situations. Others might have a better angle than you—rapidly adopt their insights.

The quality of your judgment is shaped by the information you glean from diverse vantage points. Different people can add to your decision because they have a distinct vantage point.

Leadership Efficacy

Leaders are judged on their efficacy. *Efficacy is simply the power to produce an effect.*[2] We consider the efficacy of a drug to produce the effect we expect. High leadership efficacy is the confidence to create what matters most to the organization. Low leadership efficacy leaves you and others guessing.

To improve your leadership efficacy, position yourself at a favorable vantage point. Strategic shifting combines strategy with the psychology of advantage-making to improve leadership efficacy.

In the face of adversity, leaders take a stand; if they don't, they begin to lose their influence. How you take that stand, when you take that stand, what the stand is, and the strategy you create determine your leadership efficacy. Taking a stand without a vantage point leaves you vulnerable.

When you are in a position of power and authority, you are being observed. Recall how well Rudy Giuliani, former mayor of New York City, performed during the September 11, 2001, terrorist attacks against the United States. Giuliani tells us that he didn't become a different leader on September 11.[3] It was natural for him to take a stand because of the clarity of his vantage point. On September 11, he got it right.

Leaders need to get it right sooner rather than later, or they won't be leaders for long. A superior vantage point can help establish the four pivotal contributions of leadership— direction, protection, action, and intention for the organization. Followers expect leaders to go in the right direction, influence others to go along with them, have sound judgment, resolve conflicts, and make the right moves. These qualities are easy to recognize but difficult to do well. Leaders who do so are viewed with great appreciation and admiration.

We continually hear complaints about leaders who display these behaviors:

1. Don't provide direction, or keep changing and don't know where they are going
2. Don't resolve conflicts, so people and the organization's future are not protected
3. Don't position the company to take appropriate action when it needs to be taken
4. Don't have strong intent but are reactive and cause a crisis mode of operating

The cost is wasted efforts, delays to market, lowered morale, reduced growth, and an insufficient bottom line.

Gain Leadership Advantage Now

1. Provide *direction*—Help people know what the target is and specifically how they can help get there.
2. Provide *protection*—Develop strategies that will protect the organization and people from competitor moves. Protect the people internally by resolving organizational and people conflicts sooner rather than later.
3. Manage the *action*—Momentum management aligns the organization and makes resource decisions that keep the organization moving forward.
4. Establish strategic *intention*—People should know what matters and the key drivers that will enable you to grow rather than be in a reactive crisis mode.

Not Change for Change Sake

Jumping on the bandwagon and changing just because things around you are changing is not strategic shifting. When you follow clichés about change, you can overlook the reality of your situation. Shifting should be by design instead of from getting lucky. Luck is always welcomed, but leaders don't have the luxury of happenstance turning their way; too much is riding on it. Although strategic vantage points might lead you to solutions that are contrary to expectations, the important point is sound judgment. Counterintuitive solutions are not the objective; the objective is sound judgment that leads to a profitable course of action.

What Lens Are You Using?

Most managers look through a linear lens, but strategic shifting moves the vantage point. Just as a microscope or telescope enables you to see what you can't see with the naked eye, a dimensional lens enables you to spot what others don't know to even look for to reveal behavioral opportunities and organizational movement.

Each dimension—time, interaction, perception, and structure—is a lens that establishes a commanding vantage point to spot opportunities, create advantages, and influence outcomes.

For example, while working with Ken Kec, National Sales Vice President for HBO & Co., we applied a dimensional analysis to a problem and discovered a way to transform a $200,000 deal into a $2,000,000 deal. The company usually focused on making an immediate sale. However, the executives stepped back, looked at their customer's business, and saw a larger impact for their products and service. Instead of just fixing the customer's immediate problem, their customer agreed to buy a product that helped grow its own business. This accounted for the larger $2,000,000 deal.

Our tendency is to take the first positive answer. This isn't necessarily a bad strategy, but shifting enables you to see how you could lure a larger bounty.

Where Do You Look for Answers?

Doing something bigger is not always the solution. You want to perceive the right thing to do. Sometimes the right lens is to zoom in for a small first step; getting a foot in the door is exactly right for the situation. Most people get stuck on a formula and can't shift their thinking. If the formula works, use it. But if you can't adapt rapidly to changing circumstances, you might become toast.

Nasrudin is a holy man in many Sufi mystic tales.[4] He is the Yogi Berra of his time. In one story, he loses the keys to his home. He is on his knees outside looking for them when a neighbor happens by. The neighbor does the neighborly thing of helping to look for the keys, but after some time without success, he asks Nasrudin, "Where exactly did you lose your keys?"

Nasrudin replies, "Inside my house."

"Then why are we looking for them out here?" asks the exasperated neighbor.

"Because there is more light here!" Nasrudin answers.

Why in the world would anyone do this, and how does it apply to our discussion? Nasrudin, the wise man hidden in fool's behavior, teaches us by exaggerating the folly of our human tendencies. His apparently "crazy" action informs us of what not to do. We look for solutions where we think it will be easiest to find the answer, instead of looking in the place where the solutions are. Where are you looking for your answers?

A Dimension to Notice

We can become stuck in our formulaic thinking instead of moving to dimensional thinking. Imagine a fanciful reality in which you meet a two-dimensional being. Your task is to inform the two-dimensional being that you are a three-dimensional being and can see things differently—you see differences that would be helpful for them but they can't see it. From their flat space, they see only two dimensions and interpret everything from that perspective. Surely, you would get exasperated trying to convey simple ideas. I'm sure you have these analogous conversations with your colleagues on some issues. Edwin A. Abbott wrote about this very notion in the nineteenth-century classic *Flatland*.[5] When you encounter unworkable solutions, remember you may be overlooking a missing dimension.

Solomon's Dimensional Vantage Point

In ancient times, King Solomon was reputedly a man of great wisdom and judgment in leading his people and resolving conflict. Solomon's thinking provides clues to advantage-making for modern leaders.

One of the more famous illustrations of his judgments, a judgment that goes contrary to expectation, is the decision he made between two women claiming to be the mother of a newborn. Because there was no clear way to substantiate the claim (no DNA testing was available in those times), Solomon declared that the only right thing to do, the unthinkable, was to divide the baby in half and give each mother part of the baby. This ludicrous judgment immediately had the real mother aghast and sobbing. She relinquished her claim of motherhood in order to save the baby's life, thereby revealing her true maternal nature. Solomon interceded, knowing that the real mother's true love for the baby would not allow the unthinkable act, and Solomon granted the real mother her baby.

Organizations and their leaders typically don't need to make such profound ethical, moral, and emotional judgments as the survival and rightful maternity of a child. Nevertheless, we would do well to acquire Solomon's judgment and wisdom of the ages for our own unique situation. Solomon obviously wanted to do the right thing for the baby and the rightful mother. How do you determine the right thing to do under uncertainty and doubt?

Solomon's judgment, while ingenious in design, was profound in its simplicity. The only way to generate his solution required a dimensional view of the argument. From that vantage point, he was not caught persisting with conventional thought. After he pronounced his judgment, his followers observed the effects and could also see clearly.

Look closely, and you will see a leader who did not have the answer within him. Look closely, and you will see a leader who was not caught in the rut of convention. Look closely, and you will see someone who observed the interaction of the players. Look closely, and you will see an Advantage-Maker.

Solomon's thinking contained four options or judgments:

1.   Baby goes to mother A.
2.   Baby goes to mother B.
3.   Baby goes to someone else entirely.
4.   Baby compromise—you take the baby on weekends.

Some compromises work, but others are terrible. This was not a time for compromise. Only one mother gave birth to the baby. It was not the duplicate conception.

Seeing Beyond the Obvious

Solomon could see something other than the obvious. His ability to shift from the stories being told to a commanding vantage point enabled him to see the nonobvious. Perhaps it might be more appropriate to say that he could see what was hidden from common view. Two processes were at work:

1. **A linear thought process**—Most of us would have been caught in an "either this or that" approach.
2. **A dimensional, nonlinear approach**—This required doing something different. By shifting, Solomon could see how different options might work, and he could consider expected and unexpected solutions. Navigating through the possibilities enabled him to try something unconventional, to think the unthinkable.

A series of questions must have led him to the radical solution.

1. What actions would a real mother take?
2. How would the real mother respond to losing the baby?
3. What would make the real mother give up the baby?

Without the vantage point that enabled Solomon to find another way, the jaws of defeat would have taken their toll. This is true for today's leaders as well. Although anecdotes of ingenious kings from long ago and far away are intriguing and might help point the way, today's challenges are both similar and different.

The Neuropsychology of Advantage-Making

Shifting first occurs in our brain. Patterns of thought reflect different brain functions. No formal advantage-making brain function has been studied. However, the relationship between brain function and behavior is not new. For example, the brain's frontal region is responsible for anticipating the future and resolving complex problems.[6] We are making brain shifts. These behaviors are part of the Code of the Advantage-Maker. It's common to think "No pain, no gain"; for Advantage-Makers, it is more appropriate to think "No brain, no gain."

No Brain, No Gain

Brain-scan imagery of Advantage-Makers' brains might someday be studied by neuroscientists and psychologists to reveal how their brains function in the face of constraints. We might even find that brains want to find advantages instead of pain to achieve gain. Exercising the shifts might be exercising the brain functions for advantage-making.

Steps to Take

Shift your perception to a commanding vantage point:

1. Know the target. Fundamentally, what is most important in this situation, what function are you trying to fulfill, and what objective are you after?
2. Know what has been attempted and how it is working—the good, the bad, and the ugly.
3. Identify how the context is acting as an anchor, biasing your judgment.
4. Determine the forces at play, the interactions that are driving behavior.
5. Switch views between a close-up and a helicopter view, and to customer, vendor, investor, and employee points of view.
6. Rapidly shift to four vantage points:
   A. Instead of persisting with what isn't working, try one small step that is 180° different.
   B. Expand your behavioral repertoire; adapt to the situation rapidly.
   C. Recognize that your perception has been influenced and that you can influence others' perception.
   D. When perceptions aren't driving behavior, consider how the structure is producing the behavior.
7. From the commanding vantage point, consider the direction, protection, and action you should take, and the strategic intent you want to establish.

These steps will improve your advantage-making sagacity—that is, penetrating insight and sound judgment—to turn everything to the best possible advantage and enable you to guard against the designs of others.

The Advantage-Maker's Advice

Always, always, always find a commanding vantage point.
This will help you see past the nonsense that others say.
Be cordial, but don't be stupid.
Your judgment might be more suspect than you ever let yourself realize.
You could be jumping to conclusions.
You can skillfully handle these difficulties.
Resolve conflicts sooner rather than later.
The judicious use of power encourages followers.
You can do more about this—surprise yourself.
See the strategic context—and then act.

Tips and Tools for Cultivating Commanding Advantage Points

1. Consider your position. What is dominant—is it a local perspective, or do you have a vantage point on the current condition that gives you command over the issues?

2. Establish the practice that it is important to get it right (this is not about being perfect or being right at the expense of others), and shift up close, upside down, panoramic, etc. until you get it right.

3. Don't confuse your strength with what is right. Playing to your strengths is important; however, it might be counterintuitive to realize that someone has a better vantage point. Use that person's strengths instead of your own.

4. Independently establish your intent. Gaining independence of thought is a hard-fought battle. As appropriate, question repetitive formulas, ruts, and reactions. Do not depend on others' goodwill for your positions. (Of course, this doesn't mean you should be cantankerous or arrogant.)

5. If four different forces are at play (customers, employees, management, and stockholders), can you see things from each of their vantage points? What don't they see about each other's objectives, aspirations, and desires? Gain a close-up as well as a panoramic view, and then play out a scenario of what will happen.

6. What could you see if you were up on the "eighth floor," with a panoramic view of the situation? When you have a vantage point, consider the direction, protection, and action you should take.

7.   Can you articulate the vantage point? When you contrast individual perspectives, the overall theme might reveal a vantage point that can make a difference. If not, your vantage point is weaker, than you might realize: It might be only one point of view, so get others' input.

Chapter Recap

1. Leaders must provide the "right" vantage point.
2. The principle: Strategically shift to a commanding vantage point.
3. In *Webster's Revised Unabridged Dictionary,* the term *vantage point* is defined as follows: "A position, condition, situation, or opportunity that is likely to provide superiority or an advantage, especially a comprehensive view or commanding perspective. A superior or more favorable situation or opportunity; gain; profit; advantage."
4. An opinion is a point of view but may not be a vantage point.
5. Vantage points can be moving as well as positional. You need to include the movement of all the forces at play to see what is really going on and what is required. A vantage point is not some idealized spot.
6. Some people think wise people are smart and that's what makes them leaders. Wisdom actually develops from cultivating your vantage points. Advantage-making is derived from a commanding vantage point.
7. Many people operate according to the notion that leaders have the answer inside them. Solomon's wisdom showed us that the answers are in others as well.
8. A general assumption is that every point of view is of equal value and is valid. In contrast, vantage points are commanding perspectives for real opportunities to be found. Sometimes no one person has the vantage point, but it can be constructed by adding up the different viewpoints.

Endnotes

1. Kurt Hanks and Jay Parry, *Wake Up Your Creative Genius* (Los Altos, CA: Kaufman, 1983).

2. Albert Bandura, *Self-Efficacy: The Exercise of Control* (New York: W.H. Freeman, 1997).

3. Rudolph W. Giuliani, *Leadership* (New York: Hyperion, 2002).

4. Nasrudin tales story heard in NLP seminar, 1980.

5. Edwin A. Abbott, *Flatland, A Romance of Many Dimensions* (Oxford, England: Barnes and Noble Books, 1963).

6. Siri Carpenter in *Association for Psychological Science* 12, no. 4 (April 2005), www.psychologicalscience.org/observer/getArticle.cfm?id=1761.

PART 2
The Advantage Points: The Levers of Advantage-Making

CHAPTER 5

Adaptive Stretching: It's Not the Best Who Wins—It's Who's the Most Adaptive

Who are you going to believe, me or your own eyes?
Deny everything.
—Groucho Marx

George Prince, CEO of the innovation development firm Synectics, was a one-of-a-kind thought leader. His impact on innovation is similar to Walt Disney's impact on animation and Thomas Edison's impact on the light bulb. George understood how to innovate, and Synectics has successfully helped its clients innovate for more than 40 years; its client list is a "who's who" of Fortune 500 firms. In a conversation one evening at his home, I asked George what made him so creative. He looked at me with a twinkle in his eye (why do the wise ones have that twinkle?) and said, "I pay attention to anomalies, to the exceptions in my thinking. Most people rule out these thoughts and banish them from their attention; I am curious about them and where they might lead and what they could be."[1]

For example, George had two conversations going during a new-product development meeting: the public conversation and the private conversation. Privately, his mind turned to Hawaii. Most people would try to get the idea out of their head and refocus. George included it and asked himself, "How does Hawaii relate to developing this product?" Thinking about whales and dolphins, he tried to make a connection; their sonar communication could be a clue for developing this new sound technology product they were working on.

Appreciate Anomaly

This example illustrates a pivotal vantage point that shifts the rules of the game. Since that day, I have paid more attention to anomalies. If you do this, you will be able to see the exception in an apparent fixed position. To develop an economy of means, Advantage-Makers recognize the importance of anomaly. This helps you add dimensions and avoid ruts. Stretch yourself to find potential value in differences, inconsistencies, irregularities, glitches, and incongruities.

The First Advantage Point: Adapt and Stretch

The person with the widest range of responses wins. Nonadaptiveness is costly. Adaptability leads to unexpected control, and mental agility strengthens your position.

Managers tend to repeat familiar and reliable strategies. And why not? It worked before; it should work again. You worked hard to learn and make it work. However, new situations may require different approaches. When what worked before is no longer applicable, your strength can become a liability. You can become trapped by your competency.

Advantage-Makers face this nonadaptiveness challenge directly. Andy Grove, Chairman of Intel, has a long, successful history of dealing with, and adapting to, new and challenging situations. Advantage-Makers must vigilantly examine their mind-set for premature closures.

Tall River Weeds

Conclusions are sometimes premature, as we see in the movie *The African Queen,* with Humphrey Bogart and Katherine

Hepburn.[2] Bogart owns an old, dilapidated riverboat, the *African Queen*, held together by wit and tobacco spit. They need to get from point A to point B along the river to defeat a German Imperial Navy gunboat. They encounter enormous hardships and treacherous obstacles, but they prevail, only to be stopped deep in the river's tall river weeds. Literally stuck, they can't go on. Their destination, the Big Lake, is now impossible. The German gunboat will continue to control travel and commerce. Not a good thing. They have lost. In despair, they drink away their sorrows and fall into a drunken sleep.

Lost souls. While they sleep at night, it rains, and the rains raise the river's waters and the *African Queen* riverboat along with them. As they awaken, they can now see above the tall river weeds, and 25 yards in front of their eyes is the Big Lake. Spirits soar once again. The movie continues forward, overcoming adversity to triumph.

Getting caught in the tall weeds, managers often miss opportunities because they drop out too soon, believing solutions aren't possible. They keep their bodies in the game but drop their minds out of the game. They've given up playing to win; resigned to the idea that things won't get better, they do what they can and collect their paycheck.

What's a lost soul to do?

Adaptability and Advantage-Makers

Enter the **Law of Requisite Variety**, developed by cybernetician W. Ross Ashby. This is my favorite law, the one you can apply without legal counsel. The legislature will not rescind the law. It's to your advantage to become fluent in it and apply it skillfully.

The Law of Requisite Variety

The internal diversity of any self-regulating system must match the variety and complexity of its environment if it is to deal effectively with the challenges posed by its environment.[3]

That's a mindful. At first, this sounds like an abstract notion. Let's take a closer look. In our case, the self-regulating system is humans—Advantage-Makers, in particular.

Alternatively stated, the Law of Requisite Variety states that *in any system, all things being equal, the individual with the widest range of responses will control the system.* If leaders are to control their business, they must find ample opportunities to create value and have sound judgment. They must continuously expand their behavioral adaptability.

The widest range of responses to a problem is not just alternatives or more options. No matter how many alternatives and options you have, if they all come from the same perspective, it won't work. You need to shift to another vantage point, perhaps one that is less reactive, to find a workable solution. The kind of responses you are looking for are generated by adaptability and anomaly.

Consider an example: Two sales representatives go to the same foreign nation to sell shoes. One salesperson calls headquarters and says, "The people here don't wear our kind of shoes, so I'll be returning on the next flight." The second salesperson calls in to say, "Send all the shoes you have; the people here have never worn our shoes, so the market is wide open!" Although either salesperson's conclusion could be wrong, the second sales representative has the requisite variety in his or her behavior to succeed in these circumstances.

Stated differently, the "message" in the law is, if what you are doing is not getting you the outcome you want, do something different. Shift your thinking to a new vantage point, and create new choices.

Adapt or Die

Resistance is a waste of time.

In any situation, the person or team with the most requisite variety wins!

Sticking to what worked before can lock you in and prevent you from succeeding. What worked before might actually be inadvisable for a new project. Leaders must balance their expertise with an experimental mind-set to continue to contribute as Advantage-Makers.

Anomaly Exercise

Curiosity killed the cat. But the cat had nine lives.
Take five minutes and let your mind wander and wonder, expecting the unexpected.
When you were a kid, what were you curious about?
In your current task, what are you ruling out?
Consider an unexpected approach. If you didn't find any novel solutions, it's okay. You still have eight lives.

Big Blind Spots and Minimized Opportunities

"Heavier-than-air flying machines are impossible." Lord Kelvin, President, Royal Society, 1895

"Everything that can be invented has been invented." Charles Duell, head of the U.S. Patent Office, 1899

"The radio craze ... will die out in time." Thomas Edison, 1922

"While theoretically the television may be feasible, commercially and financially I consider it an impossibility." Lee DeForest, inventor of the Audion tube, 1926

"I think there is a world market for about five computers." Thomas Watson, chairman of IBM, 1943

"There is no reason for any individual to have a computer at their home." Ken Olsen, President, Digital Equipment Corp.

Smart people can get it wrong. Before it was proven, the Earth was still round. But how can we be so shortsighted?

Advantage-Makers Balance Expertise with Experimenting

Ingenious solutions have been developed by people who saw what others thought could not exist. Some had big visions, while others had a narrow focus. Both groups had a willingness to experiment. Advantage-Makers are experimenters.

Experimenters are willing to try things. Their natural tendency is to explore ideas, tools, and perceptions. They want to create, to bring into the world something that hasn't existed. Advantage-Makers share this underlying tendency for experimenting. Do managers?

That's a tall order for managers, who are supposed to control things. Managers become experts. They prevent wrong decisions. When confronted by new environments, experts apply their existing knowledge. In situations where their expertise doesn't apply, they are left with knowing a lot about what is of little importance. Niels Bohr said, "An expert is a man who has made all the mistakes which can be made, in a very narrow field."[4]

Before managers became experts, they were experimenters and made mistakes. Difficulties arise when experts stop experimenting. Most managers do not think of themselves as experimenters.

Advantage-Makers balance expertise with experimenting. If you are not an experimenter, this is the first step to take as an Advantage-Maker. In the midst of business uncertainties, adapt and respond to anomalies.

The content of your experiments doesn't matter; what does matter is your flexibility to move your thoughts, your vantage point, to the place that produces results. Experts have a particular vantage point. Experimenters are able to move their vantage point to see the essence of the situation.

When America landed on Mars, it wasn't in something resembling a spacecraft, but a bubble. The landing craft looked like a bunch of grapes wrapped together. We didn't land on Mars; we bounced onto Mars. Instead of a safe, smooth landing, we had a safe, bouncy landing. NASA engineers are both experts and experimenters. Without their experiments with new devices, we would not have received "out of this world" photographs of extraterrestrial landscapes. NASA engineers and managers are brilliant, and in the face of what is unknown, they took a risk.

Most of us become risk-averse because we believe what we don't know can hurt us—therefore, we stay away from the unknown.

Advantage-Makers have a different framework—what they don't know can't help them; they explore and move toward what they don't know.

Fight the urge to act as if you know something that you don't—it will misguide you. Recognize what you don't know, and explore it. This will help you spot opportunities others don't.

Fixated on Function

We get fixated on the function of a tool or process, thinking about only what the tool is historically supposed to be for, or how it functions. Lamps were used to provide illumination.

Now lamps are designed for aesthetics as well as light. We become prisoners of familiarity about our tools, concepts, and systems.

When NASA first started sending up astronauts, the scientists quickly discovered that ballpoint pens would not work in zero gravity. To combat the problem, they spent a decade and millions of dollars developing a pen that writes in zero gravity, upside down, on almost any surface, including glass, and at temperatures ranging from below freezing to 300° Celsius.

Another solution was to simply use a pencil! Develop relevant technology based on the real task. For what they needed, a pencil worked.

Jack Nicklaus built many golf courses, but the challenge on the Cayman Islands was to build a smaller golf course due to the size limitations. He found a solution to the Islands' "smallness" constraints by breaking the fixation on the golf course. Nicklaus shifted his thinking from the golf course to the golf ball. He designed a ball that wouldn't travel as far when hit. Golfers continued to have the same golf swing as on any regulation golf course. Nicklaus shifted his vantage point and found a different dimension to leverage.

Encouraging mental agility helps you spot the unexpected. To do so, you need to stretch yourself and cultivate your curiosity. You need to be a tracker. Reset your fixed mental sets, and use anomaly to your advantage.

A Young Leader's Lament

When my son, Zach, was eight he had this to say on leadership.

Zach on Leadership:

The leader is Zach. He gets everything he wants. Everyone has to bow down to him.

He doesn't have to go to bed today at 9:55 p.m., but his Mom is forcing him to and he isn't tired.

And he is never going to be tired. I think his Mom should give up.

Voila!

Zach on Leadership 2 (Several Months Later):

Zach gets a fortune cookie; it says: I am the master of every situation!

Zach concludes: The leader controls.

He immediately directs his sister, Samantha, "I command you to stop!"

Samantha emphatically sets him straight, "Get away."

As a postscript to these interchanges:

Zach, now a college freshman, calls Samantha for advice (requisite variety at work).

There is hope!

Clearly Zach has adapted and shifted. He realizes that to succeed he has to do things differently. Instead of trying to control his sister, he's adapting and therefore has a higher probability of success. Don't we all.

Chief Leverage Officer

Requisite variety results in leverage. A company's chief leverage officer is a master of requisite variety. Every advantage-making leader should have functional expertise as the chief leverage officer to

- Get the most out of everything they have.
- Create an increased means of accomplishing their aims.
- Achieve maximum effectiveness with the least effort.
- Push the envelope and harness people's ingenuity.
- Exercise their flexibility and do more with less.
- Value functional elegance in solutions (simple and precise to produce superior outcomes).
- Have an economy of means in thought and action, and continue to develop this economy of means in everyday interactions.

Survival of the Most Adaptive

For an example of a real chief leverage officer doing the right thing and creating advantages, consider Barry X Lynn, CIO at Wells Fargo bank. He implemented one of the fastest change programs in the industry. Problems with technology and ATMs occurred during the change. Customer service was reduced, and negative stories in the local newspapers weren't just on the business page. As mentioned earlier, Barry referred to this task as changing a tire on a car moving 90 miles per hour on the freeway.

The CEO of Wells considered slowing down the change effort to reduce all the heat Barry and his department were getting. Barry said, "No way. I think we should go faster. People will complain in either case. They'd be miserable if we did this to them for three years or nine months. Why not get it done faster? They'll be a lot happier if we get this done in nine months." Barry's mental agility to frame the situation accurately led to going faster and ultimately pleasing the customers and stakeholders.

He often said that it's not the technology that's difficult; it's the people and organizational aspects that are really tough. Dealing with the challenges that change brings and adapting rapidly is the most difficult factor.

Common sense would have slowed down. Uncommon good sense—go faster. All the people who worked for him knew it was the right thing to do. Barry's agility and efficiency of thought are telltale signs of the Advantage-Maker's first Advantage Point: The person with the widest array of responses wins. Barry is both an expert and an experimenter.

Do the Math on the Situation

One of the elements from the Code of the Advantage-Maker that Barry employed is "Doing the strategic math on the situation." He anticipated the possible outcomes and realized that, under the circumstances, complaints would be voiced whether the changes were made slowly or quickly. Based upon that, he made a judgment call.

As with many Advantage-Makers, Barry can size up a situation efficiently. He is an efficient thinker. Guided by the possible outcomes, he was not overloaded by the amount of information, but rather realized that if they went slower, the solutions would have one of three outcomes: make things better, the same, or worse. And if it made things better it would only be temporary. Given the reality, he did the math and decided to move forward faster in the midst of formidable constraints.

When you can see the actual options for action in a situation, you can get the most meaning from the least amount of information. Adapting this thought process enables you to do the strategic math on situations rapidly.[5] *Instead of expanding your thinking, you might need to limit it!* Ironically, your judgment will be more precise, and you will more quickly deal with difficulties.

Organizational life becomes much less complex when you can do the strategic math on the situation. Inefficient thinking can cause you to not take action or to take ineffective action.

Adaptive Maps

All leaders have mental maps that guide their specific thinking and behavior. Personal maps might be implicit and taken for granted. An invisible lever that can greatly assist leaders is a map for how to handle change. Mishandling change can be traced back to their leaders' mental maps. For example, a Vice President of product development had a strong, unconscious tendency to wait for agreement from other executives in choosing new hires. This sounds sensible. Yet upon closer reflection, the company required fast movement. He knew who the right person was, and waiting cost the company time and the possibility of losing the candidate. Recognizing that his map was limiting his effectiveness and resulting in substantial delays, he updated his map and solved critical issues sooner.

Shifting Gears

Think of your organization as if it were a car taking you to your destination. You've invested in a high-performance engine, quality in every aspect, designed to give you an exquisite ride and respond quickly and efficiently to any circumstance you might encounter on the road. You are proud of your car and feel comfortable having customers ride in it. If you are in the driver's seat, the following scenario might occur.

You are about to enter the freeway. Cars (organizations) that appear to be similar to your car are speeding by you. It's time to accelerate. The car is in first gear, and you step on the gas. The car responds beautifully and propels you forward. Other cars (your competition) seem to be moving faster than usual; now you need to go faster, too. For just these types of situations, you've invested all that money in the car. Your natural instinct is to press on the gas harder. Still in first gear, the revolutions-per-minute (RPMs) gauge jumps to the yellow warning area. The car (organization) doesn't go faster, and you press down even harder on the accelerator. During all of this, you begin yelling; that doesn't seem to work. The car begins to lunge and jerk, the RPMs are now in the red danger zone, and you cannot safely merge onto the expressway. It will take all your skill and maybe a great deal of luck to keep from crashing. Shift gears, shift gears. Finally, you shift into second and then into third gear, merging with the speeding traffic.

This little constructed story is obviously fictitious. But is it applicable?

Many executives I have worked with were unwittingly driving their organizations in first gear when they needed to change gears. The consequences could be as dire as our invented story. The driver of the car, the leader of the organization, was doing more of the same, only harder, using up resources and time; the attempted solution unwittingly maintained the problem.

Leaders of organizations must be able to shift gears. Carrying our analogy further, they must be able to shift up as well as down. In some circumstances, they need to move from first-gear thinking to second-gear thinking; in other situations, the reverse is true, and leaders must downshift from overdrive to fourth, third, and maybe second gear. They need to be able to adapt to the road and traffic conditions. A leader's capacity for mental agility and flexibility and the organization's capacity to shift gears quickly are essential to advantage-making.

How Do Leaders Shift Gears?

As told in the story of Aesop's fables, the sun and the wind argued over who was the stronger of the two. How would they resolve their dispute? They saw a traveler walking down the road wearing a coat and decided to settle the issue with a contest. Whoever could make the traveler take off his coat was the stronger.

The wind went first and tried blowing extremely hard to make the traveler take off his coat. The harder he blew, the tighter the traveler held on to his coat, wrapping it ever tighter around him. Then it was the sun's turn. The sun came out and began to shine. The sun warmed up the sky and the earth, and it became progressively warmer. Soon it became too hot for the traveler to wear his coat. Off came the coat. The sun won.

Imposing your views on others can cause resistance. The harder the wind blows, the harder the traveler resists. The harder you try to force your way into other people's minds, the less likely it will accomplish your objective. In business situations, you might not be able to force your way onto your peers or boss. Customers might have a view that differs from yours. You can't force them to agree. The harder the sell, the harder the wind blows, the harder the prospect resists the sales message. Occasionally, you can win this way. Should you ever use the strong force of the wind? Of course—used judiciously, it can be essential.

Consider how the sun solved the contest. The sun set up irresistible conditions and let the person determine what he would do. Having an independent party endorse your product instead of pushing it on prospects can produce a better result. Word-of-mouth marketing works. Set it up so it is natural. The sun is not passive; it is operating on a different level of influence.

An executive dealing with a badgering, badmouthing, belittling CEO was disturbed. What to do? Quit? Maybe. Attack back with full frontal force? Not particularly workable, although it will get you a few "they've got guts" comments. Pull back and make a logical, reasoned argument, building your case with unarguable facts? You can't reason someone out of something he didn't reason himself into in the first place.

The executive did notice that the Vice President of Engineering seemed to be in good graces with the CEO. She asked how he did it. When the Engineering VP went into the field to see customers and to work with the salespeople, he made his visits contingent on the salespeople writing the CEO an account of the event. They could say whatever they wanted, but they had to agree to write something.

The Engineering VP also wrote the CEO about the customer visits with the sales force. The salespeople loved having him come out, and they reciprocated by making the case for him to the CEO.

Upon hearing this strategy, our struggling executive decided that the Vice President's method was a different tactic and began to implement his approach. She let her colleagues know that she would be involved in various business efforts and meetings with them. As part of this process, they should write a note to the CEO about the experience.

After a few months, the CEO commented that she was one of the best executives he had ever encountered. He added that he doesn't even read those letters anymore. "My hat's off to you; you've got my respect." Trying to push her case was fruitless. Letting others turn on the sun and warm up the CEO for her was simple, easy, and unexpected.

Mental Shifts

Leaders must make mental shifts. For example, NeuColl CEO Roy Fiebiger sent me a note to describe a practical shift he made in his thinking.[6]

> "This also has value in negotiations, which is something I'm doing right now. My current distributor's exclusive agreement just expired, and I've been pushing very hard—almost threatening that we're going elsewhere, etc. After our discussion this week I met with my distributor contact and took an entirely different approach. I spoke with him like an old friend. He is in a very large global organization and needs approvals from all over the world to get my deal done. So instead of pushing him further, I offered to help him accomplish whatever he needs to get done to make a new performance-driven agreement happen. He was very appreciative and gave me great detail about everything he was doing and needed to do to get a new agreement approved. I have more insight about his process and timing than before, so the approach seemed to work very well. Good chance this will happen before year-end."

The Finer Points of Requisite Variety

The Law of Requisite Variety again is "The internal diversity of any self-regulating system must match the variety and complexity of its environment if it is to deal effectively with the challenges posed by its environment."

Let's deepen the understanding of the Law of Requisite Variety and its application.

"The Internal Diversity of Any Self-Regulating System"

Humans are self-regulating systems. You can do things differently; you can make adjustments and correct course. You are not a thermostat, which can go on and off only according to a preset rule. You can reset the governor on the thermostat; challenging assumptions, you can reset the rules. You can anticipate. The capacity to anticipate is your evolutionary birthright and distinguishes you from lower primates. Besides, brains like to anticipate. Freedom and ingenuity spark Advantage-Makers.

"Must Match the Variety and Complexity of Its Environment"

Being equal to the variety of action that you encounter is critical. Having the capacity to rise to the environment's level of complexity is crucial. Versatility is like air for Advantage-Makers.

This is the where Advantage-Makers separate themselves from others. Take a deep breath, let go of the limiting way, begin to do the strategy on the situation, and flex your mind.

"If It Is to Deal Effectively with the Challenges Posed by Its Environment"

Things change and will continue to change. You will encounter difficulties, challenges, and opportunities, both anticipated and unanticipated, as a matter of course. You will be required to acquire skills and insights that you don't currently possess. It's imperative for you to be adaptive—fast on your feet and generative. Create what hasn't been created. Advantage-Makers live with no guarantees.

Requisite variety is not about positive thinking, but rather thinking powerfully, harnessing your ingenuity, and developing choice-making powers.

After his retirement as Prime Minister of England, Winston Churchill gave a speech at his alma mater, a place where he had failed several times. When asked what the key to success in life was, he replied, "Never, never, never, never, never, never give up."[7]

Churchill knew the score when he stood face to face with the odious tyranny of the Nazis' attack on Great Britain. He turned the bleakness of the challenge to an inspiration for his people: "Let us therefore brace ourselves to our duties, and so bear ourselves that, if the British Empire and its Commonwealth last for a thousand years, men will still say, 'This was their finest hour.'"[8]

A hallmark of greatness is not only recognizing the brutal facts, but also successfully confronting them. Identify the patterns and the situations that don't work. Having recognized them, get to work harnessing your ingenuity. Make the hard choices; cut your losses, if necessary; and move on. In England's case, there was no moving on; there was only the need to win. As such, Churchill called upon the English people to adapt and match the variety and complexity of the war environment to deal effectively with and gain control over the challenges posed by Hitler.

There Is a Way to Make This Work

Advantage-Makers skilled in requisite variety act with the presupposition that "There is a way to make this work." Advantage-Makers find ways that haven't been thought of yet. They seek smart people who might have an answer. They persist in understanding the circumstances; they adapt in ways of handling it.

Furthermore, requisite variety suggests that, in any system, all things being equal, the individual with the widest range of responses controls the system.

The best example of this is Mahatma Gandhi. He was a man without any official or positional authority who changed the course of Indian history and the world.[9] Gandhi was unpredictable; his actions weren't consistent with how political leaders or revolutionaries were supposed to act. He did not suffer from the perceptual bias of unchecked consistency (described in the Laws of Defeat). In the face of violence, Gandhi developed a code of nonviolence. His spiritual roots and nonviolent philosophy transformed those he encountered. Mahatmaji, as he was called by his followers, had a wider range of responses than the British authorities could use to control him. As such, he was in control—although it seldom seemed obvious.

The surprising twist on control is this: If you want control, become more adaptable. The Advantage-Maker with the most requisite variety wins.

Gandhi, Churchill, and You

Like it or not, the bar continues to be raised for leaders. To be effective at the next level, they must handle the variety and complexity of the environment. Just as kids learn to adapt to increasing complexity in their development, so must leaders progress in the challenges they encounter.

A good teacher demonstrates his or her requisite variety by changing the teaching approach for each student. This stretch requires mastery not only of the material, but of the ways people learn.

We are not Gandhi or Churchill, yet if we aspire to, we can make our own unique contribution. Each of us has the individual capacity to exercise the thought process that led Gandhi and Churchill to powerful choices and changes.

The Cost of Inaction

What are the consequences and/or costs of inaction, or of being committed to doing more of the same? When the tendency for behavior is postponing decisions and delaying actions, you need to play catch-up—not an enviable position to be in when you are supposed to be winning.[10]

Most of the airlines grind out business the usual way, yet Southwest Airlines found a way to satisfy customers and make money. At many points along the way, the airlines could have broken the continuum of doing more of the same. Ignoring the facts does not change the facts.

Harnessing the ingenuity of forward thinking is not only possible, but successful companies such as Starbucks make it happen. The other coffee makers focused on advertising jingles; Starbucks redefined the industry. How can you pay $3.55 for a cup of coffee? This must be the Twilight Zone. But those frappuccinos are great.

Expand Your Requisite Variety

Advantage-Makers expand their requisite variety in three critical areas.

First, Advantage-Makers shift strategies and tactics to create and respond to structural disruptions in the marketplace. Mini-computer leader DEC couldn't adapt its business model and missed the personal computer revolution.[11]

Second, Advantage-Makers design organizations with the requisite variety to adapt and improve their effectiveness. This leads to a performance-enhancing culture: All the numbers point to higher profitability, higher performance, higher job growth, faster stock price appreciation, greater revenues, and better net-income growth.[12] In contrast, IBM's 1980s culture and hardened mind-sets contributed to its troubles.

Third, Advantage-Makers develop their command over the situation and their emotional presence to navigate stormy interactions. Requisite variety prepares you to shift technology, strategy, products, or people.

The Wind and Sun at It Again

Sometimes the fastest way is to go slow. Sometimes the slowest way is to go fast. No hardened rules exist—only hardened minds. The crucial success factors for sustaining performance are the capacity to be versatile in thinking, be adaptive in behavior, and have the foresight to anticipate changes in the marketplace. Markets create surprise and discontinuity and are intolerant of low performers and poor adaptors. Skills in requisite variety and behavioral adaptability are not just nice to have—they are essential. We have moved from the survival of the strongest to the survival of the most adaptive.

An Old Advantage-Maker's Advice

"Why are you doing this? You don't need to—why give me this advice?"

"I do it because I want to do it. Imagine what we could create together if more people knew how to spot opportunities and create superior outcomes.

"You, however, do things because it makes you look good or you're afraid of looking bad. Your motivation depletes your power. Would you agree that there are a few people at work, maybe at home, who would like you to wise up?"

"Do I have to answer that?"

"I think you already have. All you need now is the chutzpah to do things differently than you normally do!"

Tips and Tools for Cultivating Requisite Variety

Exercise 1: The Experimenter—Priming the Pump

Identify a situation in which you stopped doing something that wasn't working and tried something different. The new approach might have worked. The important thing is that, if you failed, you failed forward; you experimented and primed the pump. Perhaps you learned something about influencing your boss, and instead of taking the action, maybe you needed to recruit a credible source to do the influencing.

Exercise 2: Your Finest Hour

Consider any current difficulty that you haven't resolved. Act as if it can be worked out. Like Churchill, how could this become your finest hour? What bigger solution would change the entire dynamic? How could you genuinely make the situation a non-issue?

Exercise 3: The Wind and the Sun

On a leadership issue, consider whether you have been the wind or the sun. Expand your behavioral repertoire. If the wind strategy isn't working, imagine how you could implement a sun strategy. If the sun strategy isn't working, discover how a mighty wind can work. How can you set the conditions for success rather than demanding it?

Chapter Recap

1. Anomalies are often the key to seeing what you haven't seen before. Paying attention to anomaly opens up the unexpected and, with it, potential solutions.

2. Become an experimenter to create ingenious solutions. Balance your expertise with experimenting. Fail forward. Your expertise can become inadequate to the new task.

3. We are often stuck in the "tall weeds" and don't see available solutions.

4. Requisite variety states that the internal diversity of any self-regulating system must match the variety and complexity of its environment if it is to deal effectively with the challenges posed by its environment. In other words, the person or team with the most adaptability wins. Gandhi and Churchill were masters of requisite variety. Adapt rapidly.

5. The surprising twist on control is this: If you want control, become more adaptable. The person with the most requisite variety wins.

6. Advantage-Makers use requisite variety to (1) adapt to a competitive-market environment, shifting its strategies and tactics in the marketplace, (2) design an organization with the requisite variety to rapidly change, and (3) increase their personal resourcefulness to shift their thinking and mental agility to handle changes.

7. Shift gears. You are wasting a lot of resources by staying in first gear when you ought to be in second or third gear.

8. Become the chief leverage officer in your organization. Make sure your organization has an adaptive culture.

9. You can't teach an old dog new tricks—maybe so, but you can trick an old dog.

Endnotes

1. George Prince, CEO of Synectics, personal conversation, 1987.

2. John Huston, director, *The African Queen* (1951).

3. W. Ross Ashby, *Introduction to Cybernetics* (London: Wiley, 1956).

4. Niels Bohr in *A Field Guide to Experts*,
    www.bmj.com/cgi/content/full/329/7480/1460?eaf.

5. Robert Fritz expands on this type of thinking in his seminars.

6. Roy Fiebiger, CEO of NeuColl, personal conversation, 2002.

7. James C. Humes, *The Wit and Wisdom of Winston Churchill* (New York,
    N.Y.: Harper Collins, 1994).

8. *Ibid.*

9. Richard Attenborough, director, *Gandhi* (1982).

10. Adam Hanft article at Inc.com, www.inc.com/magazine/20021201/
    24929.html. The business section of an online magazine pointed out
    consequences of inaction and of a demonstrated lack of requisite variety in
    thought and behavior.

11. Clayton Christianson, "Give Responsibility for Disruptive Technologies to
    Organizations Whose Customers Need Them," Chapter 5 of *The
    Innovator's Dilemma: When New Technologies Cause Great Firms to Fail*
    (New York, N.Y.: HarperBusiness, 2000).

12. John P. Kotter, James L. Heskett, *Corporate Culture and Performance* (New
    York, N.Y.: The Free Press, 1992).

CHAPTER 6

The Game Changer: If You Are in a Hole, Stop Digging and Change the Game

*Prediction is very hard, especially when
it is about the future.*
—*Yogi Berra*

If you are trying to solve a sticky problem, you don't want to unintentionally make it stickier. What do you do when commonsense solutions don't work? Answers, and the behaviors that prevent you from seeing them, are closer than you think. They are just in an unexpected place. The first step is to see the game that needs changing.

An earlier example of this was that the more you, as the boss, tell people what to do on all projects, the less they develop their own skills; the less they develop their skills, the less you think they are capable of doing the job without your input, and the more you tell people what to do—a game without improvement.

Well-meaning, smart, competent leaders mishandle difficulties. This is not done because of some fundamental flaw within themselves, but rather because their vantage point isn't relational. They listen to the problem from the wrong angle, making it difficult to act differently.

The Second Advantage Point: Be a Game Changer

Do something that shifts the game. See actions not in isolation, but as interactions between players, whether people, teams, departments, organizations, businesses, or countries. Strategically shifting 180° from the attempted solution often leads to workable solutions.

Inadequate outcomes and counterproductive behavior result from persisting in a course of action that doesn't work but that you think should or will. This pattern turns into poor results that won't change and recurrent problems that won't go away.

This Game Changer Advantage Point enables you to develop the core interaction pattern for becoming an

Advantage-Maker. As we unravel this knot of interactions, you might be surprised to see advantages that would not have been available to you without this strategic shift.

Managers' best intentions, combined with rapid patterns of interaction, obscure how their own actions unwittingly contribute to, and maintain, the problem.

The road to hell is paved with mishandled interactions.

Managers expect their commonsense solutions to work. When their attempts don't pan out, they often try again, with variations on a theme. But when it's wrong, it's costly. If your commonsense radar is providing incorrect feedback, it can lead you to the wrong actions. Similar to beached whales, the echolocation system—the clicking radar they depend on as their internal compass to navigate—has gone awry.

We are taught from an early age that when at first you don't succeed, try, try again. Persistence is a virtue, is it not? Yet when the problems themselves persist and become recurrent, you must change the game.

The more you ask your boss for permission to do something, the more he or she sees you as junior. The more he or she sees you as junior, the more you doubt yourself and ask questions—a game without end.

As illustrated here, the emphasis is not about the circumstances in which you find yourself; instead, it is about the nature of your attempted solutions—the interactions—that maintain the circumstances.

Many people value learning organizations yet keep repeating the same counterproductive patterns, inadvertently overlooking simple tactics that work. Another dimension of action is available.

Making Sticky Problems Stickier

Consider the categories of mishandling difficulties:
1. **Taking action when you shouldn't.**
    Overreacting to the other person, or doing too much tinkering.
2. **Not taking action when you should.**
    Missing the real requirements of the situation, dodging conflict, or distorting the facts. Attempts are often too little and too late.
3. **Taking the wrong action that maintains the problem.**
    Miscalculating, thinking the problem is one thing when, in fact, it is another. Another common error is doing more of the same approach that isn't working and expecting a different result.

Leaders Must Listen Differently

Leaders receive a recurring message that they must be better listeners; although that is generally true, it is insufficient to make a difference that matters. Instead, leaders must listen in a different way. When most people listen to a problem, they go on a search-and-destroy mission to determine the facts, deflect blame from themselves, and identify a solution based upon their past experience.

David and Jack have an ongoing disagreement about a project. The usual way of handling it is to determine the content of the argument and perhaps decide who really is mistaken. Content is important, and we might even see who triggered the problem, but because this is a recurrent problem, not a one-off situation, we should listen for *how the interaction is maintained*. From an Advantage-Maker's point of view, we are looking at how the pattern plays itself out. If this is recurrent, we can predict how it will go. David will persist, and Jack will respond in his characteristic way.

Listening differently means leaders must see the *interactive* nature of the problem.

Leaders must listen for attempted solutions. They might not understand why their attempted solutions are not working. Typically, habitual interactions maintain the problem. Not only are their solutions not helping, but they are digging a hole that is making things worse. They need to stop digging the hole and start filling it.

How's That Working Out for You?

Your credibility as a leader is diminished when you allow problems to persist. Without recognizing that we are digging a hole with no way out, we keep digging. The mistake we often make is thinking that because our communication is well intended, others ought to do what we expect. We don't understand why others aren't doing their part.

Ask yourself a critical question: *How's that approach working for you?* In effect, how is your strategy working? That is probably the most important question you can ask yourself to stop repeating actions that aren't working.

A major Silicon Valley firm was in a downward spiral. Unfortunately, the CEO was caught in a pattern that had worked in his last company but didn't fit this situation. After asking himself this simple question—to examine whether his approach was working—he began to see the problem with persistence.

Without strategically asking "How's that working for you?," you persist in similar approaches. If you don't listen differently—seeing the interactive nature of the problem—you repeat a pattern of behavior that doesn't work. You won't see that you need to do something different. Beyond stopping what isn't working, you need solutions; we discuss this topic later in the chapter. But stopping does begin something new.

An interactional vantage point sees actions not in isolation, but between players.

Your Solutions Might Not Work or Might Not Work Well Enough

Even if you sense that you must do something different, you might not see that the way you are attempting to solve the problem is what needs to be different. One of the most troublesome aspects is thinking that you are trying different solutions when, in reality, you're doing more of the same.

Consider, for example, managers who complain about resources but don't want to be seen as complainers. They make stronger arguments for their department's plight, and although they're justified in their concerns, they are perceived (unfairly, perhaps) as whiners. This approach isn't beneficial for any manager—the Rodney Dangerfield "can't-get-no-respect manager." They request more people, object to the workload their people carry, complain about their group not getting any respect from other departments, point out the inequities in resource allocation, and protest that their group is not being recognized for all its hard work. These logical concerns should be addressed. However, each time they complain, their peers see resource fights as evidence of lack of team play, and it sinks them deeper in the eyes of their boss. Instead of being problem solvers, they are problem makers.

These managers see themselves as doing the responsible thing, and in their view, they have been reasonable. Naturally, they don't want to be perceived as complainers, yet that is the characteristic behavioral signature in their problem-solving interactions. What makes this more challenging is that they don't see how their behavior has become problematic. They've become a broken record—and unless they do something different, it will soon be time to get rid of them. They won't see it until the pattern is interrupted.

Ask them, "How is your strategy working?"

Solutions do exist for solving sticky situations, recurrent problems, and anticipated difficulties, especially people-related issues. Listening differently is not repeating back what you've heard.

Listening differently is identifying the pattern of interaction that produces and maintains the problem.

Listening differently is seeing differently. When you examine the actual interaction between two people, several groups, or business competitors, you spotlight repetitive patterns that you couldn't see before.

Do Something Unexpected for a Change

In *The Origin of Knowledge and Imagination,* Jacob Bronowski asks, "Why does one chess player play better than another?" His answer is not that the one who plays better makes fewer mistakes. He says that the one who plays better makes more mistakes—in particular, more imaginative mistakes. The better player sees more ridiculous alternatives. According to Bronowski, the mark of a great player is that he thinks of something that, by all known norms of the game, is an error.[1]

You expect your original attempts to work. If what you are doing isn't working, do something different. The second part of this Advantage Point is to do something unexpected for a real solution. What should you actually do when you are in a recurrent pattern?

A manager was achieving major milestones, yet colleagues were disappointed he wasn't doing enough. He repeatedly defended his actions, pointing out all they had accomplished and further alienating his peers. The remedy was to replace his persistent pattern with unexpected agreement: "I want to do even more than you have suggested; we aren't moving fast enough. Let's figure out a way to do that." The colleagues appreciated his focus, felt they were now on the same page, and continued working toward mutually agreed upon results. He changed the interaction and their mind-set.

In other words, we are looking at the nature of the "A and B" interaction. This seems straightforward and simple enough, but let's not oversimplify it. Although this solution is easy to spot when you are listening differently, it is almost unacceptable when you are not.

By doing something unexpected, the dynamic changes. How willing are you to do something unexpected—similar to our fortress commander, the Avis "We try harder" campaign—or to be in agreement instead of disagreement?

Listening for Leverage

Advantage-Makers listen for leverage. They find the problematic interaction that doesn't work, and replace it. The replacement behaviors are solutions that contrast with the previously attempted solutions. If you have been trying to be helpful, perhaps you need to ask for help instead of pushing your opinions. First, you must see if it addresses the characteristic approach that is maintaining the problem.

Although I think most managers are of sound mind, their behavior sometimes falls prey to continuing to do what they've always done and expecting a different result. Knowing that you need to do something different doesn't mean you know how to do something different. However, you can cultivate the mental agility to find alternative solutions.

Strategic Maneuverability: A Surprising Way for Leaders to Stack the Deck

The book's opening story of defending a fortress under siege against an attacking army is an even more formidable, stressful challenge than a business coming under attack in today's uncertain economic times. The commander changed the game, and the outcome was far better than expected for those who couldn't see the design of the maneuver. He was at a disadvantage, down to his last few resources, and he still outmaneuvered his superior opponent. He had to do something different.

Doing something different might be a simple shift, or it might require something unexpected. Cultivating this ability to produce solutions that others don't see requires an appreciation of strategic maneuverability. At times, the difference can seem illogical from the point of view of the initial problem. The fortress commander seemed completely illogical in his solution. The unexpected message could have been developed only by stepping outside the established logic of the battle.

Different doesn't mean wild, although it might seem illogical from the perspective of the original problem. The rest of the chapter provides both direction and unexpected solutions to difficult recurring problems. Changing the game reveals hidden opportunities.

Change the Music

Here's a clue: Listen to the music. The more you do "x," the more the other person does "y." It's a dance. Each dancer keeps the dance going, for better or for worse. You might not even realize you are on the dance floor. Have you ever experienced difficulties in the organization that kept you up at night? Somebody needs to stop the music—or, better yet, change the music so you use a different dance step.

If you continue the dance by doing more of "x," your "dance partner" will continue doing "y." If you do less of "x," or do something different than "x," your "dance partner" can reciprocate. If you know only one dance step, it's going to be a long night.

Advantage-Makers at Avis employed the Game Changer Advantage Point. Although logical approaches strategize to win, their design was to be number 2. Had they lost common sense? Initially, they must have thought they were crazy to contemplate a strategy based upon "we are a loser"—we're number 2; we try harder.

Yet if they continued to do what they had always done—what everyone with common sense does—expecting a different result, they faced bankruptcy. Furthermore, they wouldn't have been able to afford the psychologist fees to deal with their insanity of doing more of the same but expecting better results.

In their book *Change,* Paul Watzlawick, Dick Fisch, and John Weakland describe the attempted changes of someone who is having a nightmare. Running faster or hiding doesn't stop the bad dream. That's just doing more of the same. The faster you run, the faster the monster runs after you. Trying to change the situation at the same level as the dream is a *first-order level of change.* The more you do it, the more it stays the same. To actually stop the nightmare, you wake up. They refer to this as *second-order change.*[2] In a second-order change, the logic of the problem no longer exists.

When you are awake, you cannot be having a nightmare. You are no longer bound by the dimensions of the problem; you are, in effect, living in the dimensions where the solution exists.

Things that don't fit with the expected logic are called illogical. They are outside the usual, outside the logic that holds the problem together. Our fortress commander and executives at Avis used logic that was second-order. It didn't keep the dance going; it changed the rules of the dance. Our upside-down thinking might need to change to succeed.

Insanity: Continuing to do something that doesn't get you the result you want and expecting things to be different.

We've looked at two demanding environments—a fortress under siege and a business on the verge of bankruptcy. What about the direct demands on senior executives?

"I'm at My Wit's End—Now What?" A President's Question

"I'm at my wit's end—now what?" asked the President of a leading corporation. The President had recently been given negative feedback about his own performance from the CEO, and he was recounting this to me, his leadership advisor. Employees told the CEO confidentially that the President was arrogant, unapproachable, intimidating, and noncollaborative. They couldn't trust him, and he often dismissed their ideas as ludicrous.

The President's frustration was palpable; he was distressed and concerned about the impact of his perceived dysfunctional personality on the organization. He didn't see himself this way. In fact, he was a top performer, contributing to the financial success of the organization. He prided himself in aligning the organization to move forward instead of wasting money and spinning its wheels in unnecessary delays and conflicts. He worked diligently to get everyone on board and to keep momentum going.

He was stunned and confused by the feedback. Yet, as a good corporate citizen and a results-oriented problem solver, he knew he had to take action, so he went to work trying to correct the situation. As you will see, he seriously considered leaving a highly lucrative position.

Attempted Solutions

The President understood that he needed to be more collaborative, but he didn't understand the specific issues that had to be addressed and who was having the most heartache. He thought that whatever the cause was for the "bad rap," he could fix it. Over the course of a month or two, he tried working with the CEO to get some answers so that he could take effective action. The discussion of the strategies he attempted and the results of those approaches prior to my involvement are included next. Then you can see the recommendation, the suggested actions, the results, and a dimensional analysis of the vantage point that led to success.

Initially, the President used what I characterized as a "going on a hunt" strategy, inquiring into who, what, where, and when. He asked the CEO to tell him who said what so he would know who needed to be addressed to make the situation better. The CEO appropriately responded that the information was given to him in confidence and, therefore, he could not reveal their names to the President. The CEO had assured the employees that he would provide the appropriate protection. The people felt intimidated and feared retribution if they spoke directly to the President about their concerns.

"How did the 'hunt' strategy work?" I asked. He had tried this numerous times, in several ways.

"Not well," he said, exasperated. Each time it had been rebuffed. The CEO simply provided him with the negative comments he had received—washed of any identifying factors.

"Then you don't want to do that anymore," I suggested. "What else have you tried?"

"Since I don't know who, when, or under what circumstances, I can't do anything," he said. "I told him, 'It's your problem, Mr. CEO! You just tell me specifically what you want me to do, and I'll just do it. General terms are too abstract and are not working.'"

This strategy is referred to as "return the volley." He was trying to give the task back to the CEO to fix. It was not typical for the President to push back like this; he usually pushed through difficulties until they were resolved. Yet he couldn't figure out what to do, so he tried what he thought was this really different approach.

"How did it work?"

"Not well." Disappointed, he added that the CEO had reiterated the principles of collaboration and said that he knew the President would do his best to reduce the employees' fear.

"Then you don't want to do that strategy anymore, either," I said emphatically.

"What else did you try?"

"Basically wait it out." We referred to the third strategy as "Do nothing."

"And the results?"

"That didn't work either" he said. "All it has done is put me at my wit's end. I'm stewing in this dumb situation. I'm seriously thinking of leaving the company; it will be a huge loss to my career and future. This position and compensation are excellent, but this situation is undermining my ability to work productively, as well as sleep. It's just not worth it!"

"So you have three strategies that you have attempted, and none of them has made any significant difference. Let's not do any of them again."

"Okay, so what should I do?" he exclaimed.

What's Really Going On

In characterizing the President's strategy, it basically was an "attack and defend" cycle. He was either attacking or defending. Neither of these patterns had worked or would work.

Let's quickly review the strategies:

1. **Go on a hunt**—Who said what? I need to know to make it better.

2.   **Return the volley**—It's your problem. Tell me what to do.
3.   **Do nothing**—I'm at my wit's end.

      His attempted solutions were, in fact, counterproductive. They reinforced the perception that he was arrogant, intimidating, and noncollaborative. A cycle developed: The more he attacked and defended, the more the CEO poured it on. This produced unintended results and unexpected consequences from the President's point of view. He was just trying to logically solve the problem. Moreover, he had tried several different ways.

      His strategies hadn't worked, and he didn't see that persisting in them was maintaining the problem. The patterns of interaction were now predictable. If this were a movie and you were a member of the audience, you could predict what would trigger the sequence and how the conflict would unfold. "Here we go again" would be an expected buzz in the movie theater.

180°—An Unwitting, Game-Changing Solution

      Let's step back to a commanding vantage point to observe the pattern of interactions.

      "The attack-and-defend strategies haven't worked and won't work," I told the President. "The more you 'attack and defend,' the more things stay the same." I explained the counterproductive pattern, and the President agreed.

      "Let's do something unexpected that might work," I suggested.

      "Okay, what?" His frustration was obvious.

      "The next time he gives you the list of complaints, *sympathize* with him about the extra burden he has taken on to fix this collaboration problem. In fact, be *supportive* of him—say something positive. Tell him that you recognize how much he is doing strategically for the organization, that that's a big job and that you are sorry about this added workload. Ask him, 'How is it affecting you?'"

The President immediately laughed derisively and said that was the stupidest advice he'd ever heard. "The CEO wouldn't and shouldn't want to hear that, and I don't want to say that. We are busy men and have to be productive."

This idea obviously was beyond his usual way of thinking; in fact, it assailed his logic, and he said so. He needed some influencing.

"Hmm, really? What's wrong with being supportive of him instead of attacking and defending?" I asked. "You don't dislike him, you know he's competent, and this is not about kissing up. We already know your attempted strategies aren't working, and you wanted to do something to influence the situation and demonstrate your willingness to collaborate."

He sat back in his chair, blinked twice, and became pensive.

"Well, when you put it like that, nothing. Hmm, I guess I could do that.... Okay, I'll try it. I've got nothing to lose."

Two weeks later, as I walked down the executive corridor, the President saw me and said he had to talk. He asked, "Did you talk to the CEO?"

"No, we've both been busy." (He thought I had been working behind the scenes to smooth things over, which I hadn't.)

"Well, it's a miracle! He walked into my office and started complaining, and I did as we had rehearsed. He stopped unloading on me and appreciated my comments, and we had the best conversation that we've had in years! We are really on the same page—we worked out what had to be done, and we are working effectively on these issues. That was the best advice anyone has ever given me. My wife thought it was good advice as well."

Case Epilogue

The Vice President of Human Resources told me several months later that the President was really setting a collaborative example while maintaining productivity. The Game Changer Advantage Point enabled us to examine the President's logic that maintained the counterproductive pattern of interaction. Shifting his logic and interaction 180°, from attack and defend to support, established a new interaction pattern. The President had changed from being at his wit's end—and about to leave or be fired—to keeping his job, collaborating more.

Your Option

Most managers confronting problems think they are adaptive, flexible, and willing to try different ways to get results. Yet under closer examination, managers inadvertently employ strategies that might seem different but that result in the same unworkable outcome. Each of the President's attempted solutions seemed different from one another. Predictably, the more he maintained his approach, the more the problem persisted. The attempted solutions became the problem. Doing more of the same, harder, simply doesn't work.

So what does work? How do you stop mishandling these difficulties? What is the advantage-making strategy? You do something substantively different. But how?

When confronted with recurrent conflicts that seem intractable, you can create unexpected solutions in these ways:

1. Identify the attempted solutions; describe how they maintain the problem.
2. Stop persisting in what isn't working—more of the same doesn't work.

3.   Think 180° from your attempted approach; design a small or big unexpected step.

Game-Changer Shift

The third point, the new solution, causes the shift. This approach works because it examines the dynamics of the interactions, the resulting behaviors, and unintended consequences. Creating second-order change or 180° shifts[3] adds an unexpected dimension.

The President, similar to most people, thought he had tried different strategies already and nothing would help. We each have a way of getting our boat from A to B and of solving difficulties—we can call what makes sense to us our "logic boat." To shift, he had to see a dimension that wasn't in his logic boat. He had to go outside the logic boat without drowning.

Admittedly, the approach is not as easy as it sounds because we are caught up in our philosophy of how things work. It takes guts to go counter to your common sense; however, when what you are doing is not working, it is imperative to not do more of the same. No perfect answer exists—only strategies that work. Counterintuitive strategies are the only way to win in the face of common sense that isn't working. They help you snatch victory from the laws of defeat.

Does this work only when there are no exits? The examples have been mostly about situations that seem to be at the last straw. Is this really just using reverse psychology on everything? That is a far too simplistic conclusion, and in reality, it makes it difficult to see what is really going on; it would reduce rather than expand your maneuverability. A Game-Changer shift is actually about how you handle difficulties.

The Super Bowl

The 1985 Super Bowl, between the San Francisco 49ers and the Miami Dolphins, was held at the Stanford University football field. The Palo Alto Police Department's chief of police had the entire security force patrolling, protecting, and preempting any trouble.[4] The world was watching the game on TV; the crowd in attendance was almost 75,000. Not enough police were on hand to cover that many people. No screw-ups could occur. They had to do more with less. Neighboring communities had sent reinforcements, but the Palo Alto police still had far too small a force to manage with the usual tactics.

On the day of the Super Bowl, the chief called in all the police and security guards for a mandatory meeting before the game. The message was clear: There would be no overreactions to be caught on national television and no strong-arm tactics, nothing that would escalate difficult situations. If the police force received national TV coverage, the chief wanted to demonstrate only positive relations with the public.

Surely similar messages are given to all police and security guards before big-stage events. In this situation, another message was sent—with flowers. All police officers would wear red carnations. Each officer was issued a red carnation to wear in his or her lapel.

Before, during, and after the game, a special group of officers replenished any carnations that had fallen out or had been lost or given away. The carnations were conspicuously placed where everyone could see them.

So what were the red carnations for? They helped present a different image: We are here to influence the situation in a positive way. As ambassadors rather than only enforcers. This was a subtle but powerful shift and message: This is a fun community day; let's enjoy it together.

While the 49ers were winning on the field, the police changed the game off the field and won as well.

Everything they did was intended to interact with the community spirit of the day—a 180° different strategy, ambassadors instead of the appearance of full force. With fewer officers, the police were able to influence a much larger crowd than normal. They did more with less in two ways. With the carnations, they influenced the way the fans perceived them. And because that perception was more positive, it engendered less negativity and thus required fewer police.

They did significantly more with less by taking uncommon action. Instead of overwhelming the spectators with their presence and reverting to hard tactics, the chief employed a behavioral strategy that transformed the way the police saw themselves. It could be argued that this allowed them to act differently, as members of the community instead of as enforcers. The fans also saw the police in a different light, and the interaction was fundamentally different.

Which perception changed first: the fans' perception of the police, or the officers' perception of themselves? We don't know. What really matters is that the positioning and frameworks for the interaction were altered. Only one arrest was made in a situation that usually involves numerous infractions that typically range from misdemeanors to felony charges.

The police chief's behavioral strategy was truly genius. Although we don't often think of police chiefs as Advantage-Makers, he certainly employed advantage-making strategies. The cops were amused and grumbled at first, but the chief held his ground in implementing his strategy. During the game, some officers appeared without carnations. Why? Well, some gave them to the fans, and that created positive relations with both the individual and the rest of the throng looking on.

Some police didn't want to keep the carnations on. As mentioned earlier, the special carnation-replenishment unit took care of that situation rapidly.

In each case, the situation was confronted with fresh eyes, fresh thoughts, and an interactional view of things. From the Game-Changer Advantage Point, you are able to see differently and, thus, think differently. To maneuver your way successfully in difficult situations, you look closely at people's actions and reactions. If A does something to B, what will B do back to A? If you do something different to B, B will respond differently to A. A strategic shift in the dynamic changes the game.

Unintended Consequences

Mishandling difficulties can lead to recurrent problems. The more we urge our kids to communicate, the more they feel we are lecturing, so they fall silent. The more they are silent, the more we lecture. The vicious cycle, from the best of intentions, is paved. Consider a few additional examples of unintended consequences.

The more an underperforming employee defends his or her behavior, the more the manager tells the employee to improve, which can lead to the employee defending his or her behavior even more. The more the employee keeps the status quo of being uncooperative, the more the manager pressures him or her to change the undesirable behavior. This game has no winner.

The more you try to get the entire team to like a new policy, not just do it, the more they argue against it—and the more they argue against it, the more you try to persuade them to like it. Compliance isn't enough in this game.

Try This Experiment

Possible solutions to each of the previous dilemmas lie in understanding the interaction pattern and, for at least one of the participants, shifting. Imagine solutions that interrupt the pattern. Consider small steps you might do differently.

Parents who care are always giving. Yet that very giving can become overinvolvement, robbing kids of growing up, getting some bruises, and learning to stand on their own two feet.

The more overinvolved the parents are, the less the kids need to fend for themselves; the less the kids learn to fend for themselves, the more overinvolved the parent becomes.

My parents provided both love and the conditions for building a backbone. One evening, my Dad was discussing paying for my college with my Mom. I was sitting nearby, so I could hear what was being said—some of the most poignant growth arrives when parents talk about you instead of to you. My Mom wanted me to have the best education to make my life easier. Neither my Mom nor my Dad had gone to college. My Dad wanted the best for me as well, but, always the Advantage-Maker, he said something that remains with me to this day: "Let him go a little hungry." The implication was, let's help him make sure he knows what he wants and that he can do what it takes to make it happen. Good move, Pop.

A New Vice President

I was working with a newly minted Vice President, and everyone kept referring to him as the "Junior Vice President." He was an amazing performer, extremely bright, and had contributed millions of dollars to the organization. Junior or not, he produced. The Human Resources (HR) people and his peers kept pointing out his oversights or weaknesses. They used a 360° instrument to assess his strengths and weaknesses to support him in his journey to being a bona fide Vice President. The more he tried to accommodate the HR folks and his peers, the more he was seen as a newly minted Vice President. He is a gracious man, and everyone likes him. He was almost taking orders from the HR manager assigned to him.

Finally, he and I realized the game as we concretely reviewed the interactions and consequences. He began to break the pattern in a most unexpected way, at least to HR and his peers. He stopped being concerned about his communications in the way the HR group wanted him to be, and he gave orders to his HR manager to shape up and do what he wanted for the business. He also spoke up and, at times, disagreed in peer meetings instead of sitting back and listening. The result, ironically, is that he is respected as a "full" VP. At this point, he is mentoring younger managers in the organization. Many wanted to know the secret that helped him, since he moved so quickly up the career ladder. His secret is rapidly shifting attempted solutions—in this case, constructive disagreement and influence replaced agreement and accommodation.

Don't Waste Your Money on Team Building

"Don't waste you money on team building"[5] was the advice Karen Schlanger, Director of Palo Alto's Mental Research Institute, and I gave to the CEO of a start-up high-tech firm in Silicon Valley. Why would we ever give that kind of advice? Not only was it counterintuitive and against the instincts of the CEO, but that's part of my professional service—helping teams produce higher levels of performance.

Difficulties were rampant in the engineering department. The engineering team, composed of several specialties, was in disarray; morale problems were high, performance suffered, and retention was a major question. The business environment was difficult, and the product was late.

The CEO and Vice President of Engineering provided the engineers with interesting technical problems, social events to celebrate small wins, and were responsive to most requests. However, things didn't improve.

These conventional solutions missed the real action that was taking place. The executives then requested a team-building exercise to improve morale, hoping that would turn things around in the organization. Again, this approach was not based upon "reading" the real situation; it was based upon opinions that teamwork would make things better. This was a quick, rational, "good enough" solution that should satisfy the situation.

In our initial assessment, we interviewed the engineers and engineering managers to understand their point of view, how things were going, and what they thought needed to be done to improve the engineering department.

We found that some of the engineers had serious personality conflicts with each other. Distrust, finger-pointing, and blame were everyday realities. As with most start-up environments, the engineers had been working really hard, but now they had no energy and were tired.

The business environment, in contrast, was booming. This was a start-up firm with about 150 employees, and the engineers wanted to cash in on the opportunity. They wanted the company to go public, as an IPO, or to be sold. Many of their colleagues at other companies were becoming millionaires "overnight." They were afraid that the bubble would burst (in this, they were right). Whenever they didn't like some decision—or somebody—they marched into one of the executives' offices and complained. If they couldn't get any satisfaction, they went to the next open door they found. Even the CFO found himself discussing technical decisions and employee complaints. He eventually escalated it to the CEO, who tried to make things work while providing business sense to the discussions. Instead of viewing these dynamics from a strategic vantage point, they reacted to the immediacy of the complaints. The company was in the grips of the "reactive" Law of Defeat.

The CEO was an unusually open-minded executive—mentally agile, strategic, and a skillful communicator. He believed having high-performing teams was the best way for companies to be productive. Improving the engineers' work relationships would be good for the business. Although he considered getting rid of some "bad apples," he knew that replacing them would be extremely difficult in the booming job market. Few resources with their technical skills were available. The company was continuously trying to recruit talented engineers. To find a solution to all this bad blood in the engineering group, he relied on what had worked in past teams; he concluded that if they knew how to function as a team, they could solve the conflicts and move forward. Sounds reasonable.

The recommendation to not do team building offsite was counter to what the executives expected. We could see it would be a waste of time and resources.

The CEO and the executive staff were surprised when we advised them to not spend money on the team-building program. As a rule, it is important to hear employees' concerns; engineers are usually good at spotting the people issues, even if they are not always skillful at dealing with the conflicts.

The executives were overaccommodating, bending over backward with an open door policy that the engineers misused. Whenever they didn't get their way, they ran to the next open door among the executives until someone took up their cause, whether or not it made good business or organizational sense. It seemed that the engineers held the upper hand because they knew it was hard to get new replacement engineers during the height of the dotcom phase in Silicon Valley.

The more they accommodated and responded to the complaints, the more the engineers escalated their requests. Threatening to leave if they didn't get what they wanted, the engineers were almost holding the company hostage to their requests. This was the unintended consequence of having an open door, willing to listen accommodation policy.

The first step was to frame the issue for the entire executive team: Their situation was similar to a family in which the kids "worked over" the parents, going back and forth between them until they arranged to have what they wanted. To change the game, we advised the staff to stop taking up individual causes and have the employees speak to one key executive when they had a complaint. They agreed to implement this strategy, and, to their surprise, the complaints reduced dramatically.

Although the engineers never told us they would leave, we predicted specific parts of the engineering department would be gone within a few months. Therefore, it would be a waste of time, money, and attention cycles to invest in a team-building exercise. As predicted, they left within four months.

Afterward, the CEO said we had provided sound advice:

- Don't throw good money after a bad situation.
- Reestablish the lines of authority and the judicious use of their power.

The executives wanted to take reasonable action and work things out with the engineers. That sounds sensible and logical. Why would you ever be against that impulse? After all, it was holding the engineering group together. Our Game-Changer Advantage Point enabled us to be concrete—not just talking about generalities such as teamwork or productivity, but defining the actual attempts and consequences of holding the group together. This revealed how the executives had inadvertently mishandled the situation. To their credit, they were strong enough to see how counterproductive those actions were for the entire organization.

Persistence Keeps You from Finding Hidden Assets

The Game-Changer approach applies to business-to-business negotiations, leadership and management, ways to do more with less, conflicts between departments, corporate communications, interpersonal issues, and, with a twist, competitive strategy as well.

Persistence, as much as resistance, is a primary culprit in maintaining the status quo. Advantage-Makers strategically maneuver to shift the game. Without strategic maneuverability in their thought processes, leaders are at a disadvantage. Exceptional leaders see what others don't by shifting to a Game-Changer strategy. You lose maneuverability when you do more of the same but harder; the extra effort won't work, and it is costly.

Forbes magazine shifted the way it approached the cost of sick pay to its opposite—wellness pay—to reduce health-care costs. Instead of sick pay for absence, they rewarded health. Employees could earn money and liked the program. The upside for *Forbes* was a 30% decrease in major medical and dental claims.

A Game-Changer action stacks the deck in your favor. If executives are to do more with less, find hidden assets, leverage their resources, win, and reduce losses, changing the game must be a key capability that they develop and employ.

The fortress commander needed to stop persisting in a strategy that didn't work and do something that, at first glance, seemed illogical. Avis Car Rental's efforts weren't working; the company needed to shift its actions and proclaim it was number 2, so their people try harder. At the Super Bowl, the chief of police had the foresight to have everyone, including the police themselves, see the police differently by wearing red carnations. The President took an unexpected turn to improve his collaboration with the CEO. And the high-tech CEO stopped accommodating a lost cause and reestablished the judicious use of power. Leadership is emboldened by shifting from first-order change to second-order advantage-making strategies.

U-Turn

In her later years, my Mom's independent spirit was supported by her reliable Toyota, a car she named "U-turn." She was living in Ft. Lauderdale, Florida, at the time that I first heard the name. We were driving to a local store when she made a wrong turn. She said, "Well, time for U-turn to do its trick." She didn't persist in the wrong direction. Simply a U-turn. She would laugh—an amused, delighted laugh, a don't-take-this-too-seriously type of laugh. Don't argue; just change directions. Oops—U-turn time; it was a charming time. This U-turn wisdom is worth recalling when you make a wrong turn. Don't persist; U-turn.

Steps to Take for Recurrent Problems

1. For recurrent problems, identify concrete, specific interactions that aren't working. Who, specifically, did what, specifically, to whom, specifically, and what, specifically, did they do behaviorally in return?

2. Identify the characteristic repetitive attempt—the pattern. Perhaps you have tried everything, but if you look closely, you might see that the attempts have a characteristic, more-of-the-same flavor that isn't working.

3. Look at each attempted solution and ask, "How's that strategy working for you?" Stop persisting in what isn't working.

4. U-turn instead of persist. Based upon what you know, shift your actions 180° or implement a small change that has worked in the past. The commanding vantage point is to see the solution in the interactions.

Steps to Take for Upcoming Situations

1. Identify what you are after and what your concern is.
2. Determine the expected way of handling these types of situations.
3. What characteristic pattern doesn't work in them? What's the logical outcome if you do it the usual way?
4. Instead of preparing to do more of the same, harder, consider initiating doing something different that may be easier, something that might be unexpected that could lead to a different outcome. This could be a 180° different strategy.
5. Try it out and adjust as you move forward.

The Advantage-Maker's Advice

Do something unexpected for a change.

Tips and Tools for Cultivating Game-Changing Solutions

1. Be specific and concrete about the interaction. Avoid generalities such as "teamwork" or labels such as "considerate of others."
2. Who, specifically, did what, specifically, to whom, specifically, and what, specifically, did they do behaviorally in return?
3. What have been your specific attempted solutions?
4. How have the attempted solutions worked?
5. Consider what might be working but that you're not noticing. Under what circumstances does the difficulty not happen?

6. What small, concrete step would shift the attempted solutions from more of the same to something different?
7. Develop pattern recognition to see that more of the same actions produce more of the same actions in the other person.
8. If you continue doing what you've always done, you'll continue getting what you've already got.
9. Think about developing a second-order change—a change on the attempted solution that might seem illogical from the framework you have been operating within.
10. U-turn—create a 180° concrete solution, and try it.

Chapter Recap

1. What do you do when common sense isn't working? If you keep doing what you've always done and expect it to be different, that's insanity.

2. Doing more of the same usually leads to more of the same—a first-order change effort. How do you stop mishandling the difficulty? A second-order change, or 180° strategy, can lead to unexpected solutions.

3. The second Advantage Point for finding hidden opportunities: Game Changer. Instead of persisting in what isn't working, do something unexpected for a change.

4. A president who mishandled employee and CEO complaints inadvertently perpetuated an "attack and defend" strategy that was inadequate to the task. He shifted 180° to a support strategy and succeeded.

5. The police at the 1985 Super Bowl wore red carnations. This changed how they saw themselves and how the fans saw them. It resulted in the fewest arrests ever for an event of that magnitude—and they did it all with fewer resources than conventionally required.

6. Unintended consequences result from repetitive cycles. For example, the more you complain, the more they tell you to stop complaining; the more they tell you to stop complaining, the more you complain about being told to stop complaining.

7. A high-tech CEO was advised not to waste his money on team building, but to change his tendency to over-accommodate. This reestablished the judicious use of his executive power.

8. U-turn, my Mom's message: If you are going in the wrong direction, don't argue; change direction.

Endnotes

1. Jacob Bronowski, *The Origin of Knowledge and Imagination* (New Haven, Connecticut: Yale University Press, 1979).

2. Paul Watzlawick, John Weakland, and Richard Fisch, *Change: Principles of Problem Formation and Problem Resolution* (New York: Norton, 1974).

3. Karin Schlanger, Director of the Mental Research Institute (MRI), describes the changes as 180° strategies.

4. Randy Rafoth, University of San Francisco Department of Organizational Studies, graduate seminar discussion, 2002.

5. Karin Schlanger, Director of MRI, collaborated on this case to frame the unexpected 180° strategy.

CHAPTER 7

Move or Lose: Manage Momentum to Advance Your Organization

Nothing happens until something moves.
—*Albert Einstein*

Advantage-making leaders advance organizations. Do you move "the ball" forward? And do you move it forward enough to score? Advancement is not just progress, but actually moving the ball forward and scoring—achieving results that are worth achieving. Your leadership efficacy increases with your confidence to produce the necessary or desired results. It is evaluated in terms of advancement, not level of effort or activity. The advancement of your organization matters, and regardless of the organization's size, the game is won or lost on movement.

What can you do to achieve the movement you want? Why do organizational change-management programs fail or have only marginal value? How are the best efforts of your leaders, managers, and employees neutralized?

This chapter addresses these movement questions by shifting your vantage point. The choices you make determine whether you advance, stay the same, or fall behind.

The Third Advantage Point: Move or Lose

Spot the invisible forces at play that drive forward movement. Use strategic moves for rapid advancement.

Penetrating to the heart of the matter and seeing the underlying structural forces driving movement in the organization enables you to create unique advantages and, at times, unexpected solutions. In both business and military endeavors, underdogs defeat much larger enemies by having better knowledge of the forces at play. This shifts the odds of success in your favor.

Advantage-Makers are keenly aware of structural forces and work with them to turn everything to the best possible advantage.

The Role of Movement

Movement makes the world go around—moving from A to B. This applies to the areas of business, nature, athletics, politics, music, literature, arts, sciences, history, and relationships.

It might not be a coincidence that we refer to civilization changers as "movers and shakers" of the world. They are movement masters.

Movement occurs at the macro and micro levels of existence. If we understand movement, we can get big things to happen from small actions.

Movement has a pace to it. Olympic athletes are running, swimming, and skating faster—breaking the old movement records. The pace of city life is distinct from country living. The difference lies in the pattern of movement.

Movement has a rhythm to it—breathing in and out. The ocean waves ebb and flow. Daylight comes and goes. We feel the rhythm of different music; different dances evolve from the rhythm inherent in the music.

Movement has a nature to it—a dynamic tension. At the movies, we get wrapped up in how the protagonists will overcome the obstacles they encounter. We want them to succeed, defeat the bad guy, find true love, discover the cure, and win. This feeling is true in everyday life as well.

Movement has a direction to it. Political movements and political parties have causes they champion and fight to make happen. Leaders find and establish the direction and thus must understand movement.

Before the initiation of action, stillness exists. At the end of every dance, the movement is finished. When movement ends, life ends.

Advantage-Makers and Movement

Advantage-Makers understand movement either instinctively or through conscious observation. Successful strategic moves are a telltale sign of a great advantage-making leader.

Your experience at work is revealed in the quality of movement in the organization. How well is movement orchestrated in your organization? As a business leader, how well do you lead forward movement from point A to point B? As adults, how well have we moved civilization forward for the next generation?

Movement is a critical element for a leader to position the organization to win.

What leaders determine to be driving movement becomes the basis of their decisions.

Structural forces drive a range of behavior within any organization, from aligned to counterproductive. Structure shapes behavior.

Forces at Play That Are Hard to See

During a strategic planning session for a high-tech start-up, inadequate sales was a major topic. The executive staff, including the CEO, CFO, Vice President of Sales, Vice President of Marketing, and Vice President of Engineering, were at the meeting to fix this problem. Each expressed reasons why the rate of sales hadn't met expectations and offered complaints about the product, engineering, and marketing as plausible explanations.

What was the real problem? Although these explanations for poor sales seemed reasonable, they missed the real force underlying the problem. Shifting our vantage point, we looked at the issue from the customer's viewpoint. Customers perceived the company as unstable. This customer de-motivator had been overlooked. Customers delayed purchases because they didn't know whether the start-up would be around a year from now. If they bought the product now, would it remain viable, and could they get support for it? When I pointed out that stability should become a strategic management objective, it prompted an argument with a newly hired executive.

The prevailing culture of this Silicon Valley organization was to be nimble, adaptive, change-ready, and innovative. These traits are desirable, especially for a start-up. The newly hired executive was adamant about the relationship between an innovative culture and product sales, declaring that both he and the culture wanted innovation, not stability, as a driving force.

Turning to Steve Little, Vice President of Sales, who was listening to the arguments, I asked what his prospects were looking for before they signed on the dotted line. Unflinchingly, Steve said, "Stability." No prospect had used that term, but it was clear from the commanding vantage point. Prospects who questioned the company's stability also silently questioned the product's longevity, making it a risky choice to purchase the product. By not recognizing this concern, management inadvertently slowed sales. After further discussion, the CEO agreed and strategically shifted organizational priorities. Stability positioned the company. To support the shift, the CEO also implemented a strategic communications program. Although the company clearly valued the progressive culture, overemphasizing it had initially clouded and misled the talented new hire's judgment. His inability to shift to the real vantage point led him to promote a failing strategy. Fortunately, to his credit, he saw the reality for the customer.

Why Make a Big Deal About These Movement Forces?

Identifying the forces at play is one of the fastest, most direct ways of determining an Advantage Point that will lead to opportunity. Shifting to the vantage point, you can see the choice between stability and innovation, and the consequences of each. In comparison, the newly hired executive had an academic concept of how the organization should operate. The "nimble" concept, although popular, wasn't contributing to business success. Targeting stability strengthened the company's offering. He didn't have a monopoly on pushing his agenda. It wasn't even a bad agenda—it simply missed the force at play that drove sales. If you want to create advantage, you want to see the real forces at play.

Consultants who don't see the forces at play are giving bad advice, and executives need better input. Their opinions are often based upon reacting to immediate circumstances instead of a strategic vantage point. When executives follow that advice, they inadvertently make errors in judgment.

Organizationally savvy leaders educate their eyes to see the nearly invisible underlying structural forces that drive behavior. These powerful forces are similar to the hidden ocean currents that drive the tides. The underlying structural forces might not be seen, but their consequences are undeniable.

In this case, the question that led to identifying the driving force was, "On what basis do customers make their buying decision?" Customers won't always know what prompts their decision. To see this force, you actually have to see the company and its products from the customer's view. This requires shifting your perspective to see yourself as the customer, experience the forces on the customer, and know what your competitors offer.

Form and Function

To recognize the structural forces, let's first consider a houseboat and a speedboat. What are the significant forces that determine behavior? The first place to look for what produces each boat's movement is the design. Each boat is designed and structured differently. You wouldn't want to live on a speedboat or race a houseboat.

As obvious as this is, the obvious often becomes illusive when we are in the middle of a problem. A vantage point enables us to see what is really driving behavior. Without seeing it accurately, we will form misguided conclusions. For instance, if the speedboat doesn't give us enough living space, or if the houseboat doesn't go fast enough, complaining about the space or the speed misses what is really driving the action.

We live at the event level—the living space and the speed. Yet if you don't see that the form is causing the difficulties, your efforts will produce inadequate results. To effectively address our complaints, we need to move to our vantage point. Winston Churchill once said, "First we shape our structures. Afterwards, they shape us."[1]

The form—the underlying structure—determines how things function. The origin of the behavior for the houseboat and speedboat is their respective structures. The form both enables and disables particular movement. If we have the wrong form or an inadequate form, we will have dysfunctional behavior or inadequate action. We need to design the structure to create the kind of movement we require—a houseboat for living, a speedboat for racing. Simple enough.

Our complaints should actually be about the form, not the behavior.

When most executives hear the word *structure,* they think organization charts and reporting structure. We can see how the reporting structure reveals some of the behavior we see in organizations. However, that isn't the full scope of what we mean by the structural force at play.

The designs we are looking at are not always physical, and they are often less visible than boats and organizational charts. With our vantage point, we look elsewhere—to the policies, decisions, objectives, rewards, workload capacity, competitive responses, adaptiveness, and other elements that form the organizational design.

Robert Fritz is the founder of structural dynamics and author of *The Path of Least Resistance for Managers.* He defines structure as "the elements in relationship to each other that give rise to behavior."[2] These elements form structural relationships that produce the organizational behavior and movement we experience. They are the structural forces at play.

In architecture, Frank Lloyd Wright asserts that form and function are one.[3] Change the form, and the function shifts; change the function, and the form must be changed. The impact on our actions is powerful.

NLP models structures that shape behavior. Change the structure; change the behavior.

Deepening Our Ability to See the Forces at Play

To understand business behavior, let's consider behavior in nature. Rivers are dynamic, yet they have predictable paths. What causes the river's predictable pattern? The water follows the riverbed—the underlying structure.

Just as a riverbed determines a river's course of action, your business has an underlying structure that determines your organization's course of action.

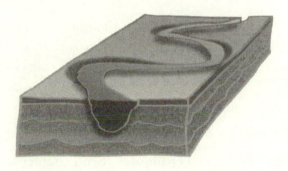

Wherever the riverbed turns, the river turns; wherever the underlying structural forces in the business turn, the organization turns.

Riverbeds can be seen, so we can see the structure that rivers follow. Highways can be seen, so we can see the structure that cars move along. Pathways can be seen, so we can see the structure that people walk along. But what about the invisible structures—the underlying structures that might be invisible to the untrained eye?

The energy grid is invisible to most of us, yet we have energy in our homes. The water system is invisible to most of us, yet we have running water from the tap. The gravitational field is invisible to us, yet the tide ebbs and flows.

To the untrained eye, the underlying structural forces in organizations are invisible. As stated previously, people in organizations tend to think of structure as the organization chart—the reporting structure of the divisions and departments that make up the company. The first thing you must do is shift your working definition. The underlying structure in organizations is the set of structural forces at play that impact, drive, and determine behavior.[4]

Business forces include competitors, regulations, economics, demographics, customer motivations, market size, and so on.

Organizational forces are the objectives, policies, cultural practices and values, accountabilities, decision-making practices, priorities, individual aspirations, and collective desires that sustain movement.

Allergic Reaction

Organizational changes that run counter to the underlying structure can cause an allergic reaction. The organization does everything it can to get rid of the alien antibody. Change efforts and projects fail because the structure rejects the change or is inadequate to support the project. Unrecognized, these structural conflicts, as Robert Fritz calls them, "neutralize your best efforts."[5] These forces are significantly underestimated as the cause of success or failure.

The CFO of a paper industry company had identified serious conflicts in his organization that were affecting performance and morale. Business was down, customers were upset, and customer satisfaction was below acceptable standards. A customer audit revealed not only that customers had their own complaints, but also that employees were complaining to the customers that other parts of the organization were to blame for the lack of service, poor quality, and delays in product availability.

The CFO had worked with the CEO to give "teamwork and pep talks" to improve morale, with the hope that they would translate into performance and profitability. His attempted solutions, although well intended, simply maintained the problem. The CEO's "play nicer, work harder, do better" dictum didn't help. Both executives were results-oriented, bottom line, action-focused managers, even though their styles differed. The real issue was invisible to almost everyone in the organization.

The CEO told me, "My business is business, not communications. I don't think you can help." The CFO was an Advantage-Maker and suggested we proceed. Together we analyzed and identified the underlying structural forces that were driving the counterproductive behavior—behavior that resulted in dissension, conflict, and poor performance. The real performance structure was invisible and unexpected to the executives. The department pay and bonus structure undermined team performance. Instead of "all for one and one for all," it was me against you, with lip service about collaboration.

If one department succeeded, the other's opportunity was diminished. Let's look at the structural interactions of three of the departments—customer service, logistics, and purchasing. The objective of the customer service group was to achieve on-time delivery while limiting complaints. The logistics group delivered the product and was measured on cost controls (for example, minimizing overtime and fuel consumption). Purchasing's task was to drive higher gross margins through lower cost and a fast inventory turn. Their respective compensations were based upon on-time delivery, cost, and margins.

So what's wrong with this picture? Nothing, so far. The trouble starts when the structure takes the steering wheel and each group takes action according to the structural objectives.

Customer service pushed to get orders delivered by certain times for customers. To meet the requests, the logistics group was pressured to change the drivers' routes and time schedules and this often required overtime pay, driving up their costs, in direct opposition to their objectives, budget and compensation.

The purchasing department bought materials in certain quantities and times to achieve good price points. Changing their buys to meet customer service requests caused price and freight costs to rise and affected inventory turnover, resulting in lower margins. Again this was in direct opposition to their objectives, budget and compensation.

The customer service promises were shifting the burden, costing other parts of the company time, money, and missed objectives. This caused serious strife between the departments because their jobs and compensation were tied to the competing objectives.

To improve performance, the executives stressed teamwork: 30% of their bonuses were based on team alignment. That meant 70% was based upon objectives that we see were undermined by the other departments' objectives. The more they pushed teamwork, the more finger-pointing increased. The logistics department's response to the call for more teamwork was, "I'm being penalized twice. First, I am supposed to be controlling costs—gas and labor—and I can't do it and satisfy the customer service requests. Second, I lose team bonus pay because the customer service group beats me up for the times I push back to control costs."

Upon seeing this, the CFO was convinced he was rewarding counterproductive, competing objectives. His initial approach had been to understand the personalities and then improve their communication.

Appropriately, he still maintained his appreciation for different personalities, but for this problem, he could see that it wasn't the right method or vantage point. Although he was surprised, he could clearly see from the new vantage point that his initial approach would not address the problem's real driving force.

Unless the company addressed the underlying performance and pay structure, words would fall on deaf ears—in fact, the CEO's attempts to do this had proved inadequate. Specific, concrete changes in objectives and bonuses to support real team alignment were initiated to shift the underlying structure, in combination with a collaboration strategy to resolve future cross-functional business issues.

The CEO continued to think this was a waste of time and resources—business is business; let's get with it. He was surprised by the outcome. The results generated $4 million in additional revenue over a two-year period, cross-functional complaints and conflicts were dramatically reduced, and customers obviously voted with their pocketbooks.

The underlying structural forces might not be seen, but their consequences are undeniable. Sorting through all the expectations of the different stakeholders helps you analyze what is important. But you need to go beyond expectations to what ultimately motivates the department, organization, and individual's behavior. You need to look at what's really moving things and what's actually getting rewarded and reinforced. Underlying forces are present in all industry sectors and in all companies.

Shifting to a Power Vantage Point

In business, the focus of movement is moving from where you are to where you want to be. You are at point A, and you want to get the results at point B. Leadership in its simplest formulation is recognizing your organization's current reality at A, while at the same time knowing where you want to get to, what results you will have created at point B, and then mobilizing the forces to move from A to B.

The following diagram depicts this movement.

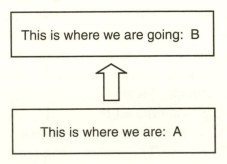

The objective is to move from A to B.[6]

The resolve of powerful Advantage-Makers is undeniable; they are resolved to create opportunities, make hard decisions, and stand up to difficulties. Strong advantage-making leaders are disciplined in their thought processes and in their actions. They generate B and recognize its relationship to A. Movement in organizations results from the decisions that are made in regard to A and B. Three movement options exist:

1. The target (B) can change.
2. The current situation (A) can change.
3. How you get from A to B can change.

What drives movement in your company? You want to get to B, so you organize to achieve that outcome. You keep your eye on the prize and make decisions about moving people, resources, and assets that support the objectives. However, the best-laid plans go astray, and conflict arises. What causes the conflict?

An Unexpected Force Produces Conflict

Let's take a look at a high-tech company that found itself in the midst of an unexpected conflict. The sales force was closing a deal, and the partnerships group was building a business alliance, all within with the same prospect—Commerce One. Neither group knew what the other was doing. Yet everything seemed fine.

The sales manager's driving focus, the objective, was to meet or exceed the quota. The strategic relationships manager was tasked with growing partnerships to expand the customer base. Both were appropriate business objectives.

The problem arose during an executive status meeting. Each VP discovered they were all trying to complete deals at different levels within Commerce One. The Vice President of Sales was focused on reaching the end of the quarter and meeting the quota. His salesperson would receive a bonus for closing this deal. The Vice President of Strategic Partners didn't want them to do the deal because it would cut into an arrangement he had been working on. The Vice President of Sales disagreed and was seen as non-collaborative, yet he was doing his job—closing the sale. Similarly, the Vice President of Strategic Partners was also seen as non-collaborative while he was trying to establish a partnership that would bring in millions of dollars. How can a Vice President of Sales be tagged as non-collaborative for trying to close a sale? How can a Vice President of Strategic Partners be tagged as non-collaborative while building a significant business alliance? Sometimes problems arise that have nothing to do with motivation, hard work, or personality.

To paraphrase Pogo, "We have met the enemy, and he is u.s. (underlying structure)!"

The CEO believed a collaborative environment could solve sticky problems. He asked me to help his executives work out the issues and find a collaborative solution.

When Collaboration Becomes a Quagmire

As expected, both sides had their viewpoint. It was my job to have a vantage point, not just a viewpoint. First, I listened to the Vice President of Sales. He had a salesperson in this prospect's company ready to close a $100,000 deal. The salesperson would make quota and get a bonus, and the VP would also make his numbers for the quarter. That's all there was to it, and he was going to close the deal. He had nothing against the Vice President of Strategic Partners; he was just doing his job, fulfilling his quota objective.

Then the Vice President of Strategic Partners stated he was hired to bring on new partnerships. He, too, had been working on an alliance within Commerce One, only at a higher level. The arrangement would require the company to give away its product for free to Commerce One. In turn, Commerce One would include the product as part of a total solution, thereby strengthening Commerce One's offer. The VP stated the partnership would rapidly increase their company's own customer base; potentially, this was a multimillion-dollar arrangement. He had nothing against the VP of Sales; they were both just doing their jobs.

Both said they were willing to work out a compromise for the future. The VPs wondered if they could figure out a system so that they would not get in each other's way. The difficulty of the situation caused them to concoct a "Rube Goldberg" scheme, one of those mazes that lampoons how to make easy things complicated. When they were done, their eyes were red. Respectfully, I told them it would never work. They agreed wholeheartedly.

The Sales VP then said that at the upcoming board meeting, it would be critical for him to have met his sales quota. This deal would make that happen. He was not going to get "beaten up" by the board for not making his numbers. He had been there in the past, and he wasn't going there again, especially because all he needed to do was close the deal.

The Strategic Partners executive also said that the board would be critical of him for not bringing on the new partnership. He wasn't going to drop this opportunity. It was, after all, good for the company.

Finding the "Right" Vantage Point

This was not a collaboration problem; the CEO had misdiagnosed it. Jeff Arnold, a certified structural consultant, said the CEO's viewpoint caused him to think situationally instead of structurally.[7] This situation had arisen between two people, so let's take care of it. The cause, from the CEO's perspective, was the situation, and the solution naturally was based upon his view of the cause. In his opinion, creative collaboration would solve everything; if this situation could be handled differently, no conflict would exist. In fact, although well intended, that approach delayed resolution and kept them from creating leverage.

Solving interpersonal conflicts requires skills and goodwill; structural conflicts require structural decisions to produce an effective resolution.

Let's shift our orientation to a vantage point where we can ask, "What about this situation makes it a structural problem?" From this position, we can see that the underlying structural forces have two competing objectives. One of the objectives will be foiled by the achievement of the other; they both can't be achieved simultaneously. Not only are they competing, but we don't know which is more important. Additionally, in terms of sequence, we don't know which should be first: sales or partnerships.

With only a few days remaining in the business quarter, the relationships with the prospect hadn't been established to make simultaneously working with them as a customer and a partner feasible. Too many pricing and timing issues existed. One of the executives was not going to meet his objectives. Neither wanted to be on the short end of the stick.

Independently, each VP's objective was perfectly sound. One was driven by alliances, the other by revenue. Alliances could cost the sales group volume on its commissions. Immediate sales could cost the company in reduced future partnership opportunities. Each executive wanted to resolve the tension by achieving his respective goals. The impetus for action is to achieve your objective.

From this movement vantage point, you can see what wouldn't work, the hard decision that was required, and who had to make the decision. It had little to do with collaboration.

The VPs were trying to solve this problem in an unworkable way and at the wrong level. The problem didn't belong at the Vice President level; it belonged at the CEO level. He had to make the decision. Strategically, he had to determine which objective was hierarchically more important for the organization at this time—meeting the sales quota imperative or acquiring new partnerships.

When the CEO looked at the forces in play, his vantage point was clearer and more comprehensive. The CEO decided to make the sale now. The important point here is not the particular hard choice; the decision was unique to the business endeavors.

A counterargument is sometimes made that it wasn't the CEO's call, but the Vice Presidents'. The VPs are paid big bucks to resolve these sticky situations, and they were shifting the responsibility to the CEO. If the problem was lack of collaboration, the VPs should have solved the difficulty, not the CEO. Although it's true that you don't want to go running to the boss for each tough decision, this decision required a hierarchical judgment.

All executives must make hard choices. What is significant here is that they must make them at the right level—it was the CEO's decision to make, not the Vice Presidents'. The conflict the CEO saw between the two executives was caused by the competing objectives, not by lack of collaboration. This often goes unseen because leaders don't shift to a lens that can see the underlying structure that is producing the behavior. Competing objectives can lead to potential structural conflicts. The underlying structural relationship was compromised. Worse, this would continue to produce counterproductive behavior in the business. The conflict between the two executives would become a battle of who had more personal power instead of what was right for the advancement of the business.

Before you think an interpersonal conflict exists, shift to see if underlying structures are prompting conflict. Resolving the actual causes of the conflict at the right level moves the organization forward.

Headwinds

Organizational conflicts must be surfaced and resolved. Leaders absolutely must resolve the conflicts between competing objectives. If you don't resolve the conflict, problems will develop, fester, and deplete the organization. Structural conflicts can stress interpersonal relationships. However, a structural conflict is not an interpersonal conflict. They need to be dealt with differently.

The tendency for conflict avoidance is more than just a personality trait; it is an organizational pitfall.

Common examples that impede forward movement are lack of role clarity and decision authority. When hard decisions aren't made, you find crisis after crisis inside your organization. Crisis management becomes more important than the original target. The movement in your organization is characterized as reactive. "Blame and defend" are daily patterns of behavior. Instead of resolving the conflict and taking action to fulfill your strategic intent, crisis management becomes the goal.

Constraints exist. Limited resources escalate tension. Engineers can't fix existing product problems for customers while simultaneously being expected to meet new product development deadlines. Inside the organization, we hear complaints about not having enough hours in the day. Maintenance and new product development are two different objectives that are necessary, but not by the same people during the same time period. Pushing harder on one side (helping the current customers) exasperates the other side ("We've got to get this new product out, but the engineers aren't making themselves available"). When the engineers work on the new product development, the existing customers complain. Then the sales force complains about not getting the products out fast enough, and round it goes.

Constraints require opportunity-generating decisions.

Good managers can mishandle the forces at play. Typically, they haven't established what is most important. People in the organization won't be clear about what to do, which results in doing less with more. Establishing the hierarchy of what is most important actually creates a commanding vantage point from which people can make informed decisions.

The surprise for executives is the extent to which the lack of hierarchical thinking causes the organization to inadvertently compete against itself. This trap is happening every day in large and small organizations. If you think that it can't happen to you, think again. It has happened to the best. Structures are powerful forces to manage. When we are in the thick of it, it is hard to see the forest for the trees.

When structures become common sense, judgment improves and profitable courses of action are designed into the organization. Analyze the underlying structure for non-obvious forces at play. What headwinds are you up against? Don't deny, distort, or dismiss the forces working for and against your objective. The forces at play are real; managing the forces separates the Advantage-Makers from the wannabes.

Do This, Not That

You need to know what really matters to you to make decisions. Steve Andreas refers to a hierarchy of importance (an NLP approach) to shape decisions,[8] and Robert Fritz's structural dynamics establishes a hierarchy of importance to resolve structural conflicts.[9] Hierarchy is an organizing principle that enabled GE to succeed in times of economic uncertainty. A hierarchy establishes the relative importance of the significant factors or forces at play. A priority list mostly tells you the order in which to do the tasks, given the time and resources. Most priority lists are really to-do lists; when everything is important to do, nothing is a priority. The hierarchy tells you the relative relationship between the different elements in a decision. In effect, it informs you, "Do this, not that," or "Do more of this and less of that."

If you can't frame issues hierarchically, you won't find leverage. When we say someone is not strategic in his approach, we often mean he doesn't think hierarchically. Hierarchy is the basis of strategic thinking, knowing the big stuff from the small stuff, and not being misled by tactical crises.

Alfred Chandler proposed a hierarchy that "structure follows strategy."[10] Establishing the strategic target is paramount; all movement in the organization adjusts to the market.

Leaders grapple with hierarchy—the good ones orchestrate it and make the hard decisions; the rest are driven by situational pressures. Mike Scott, a certified structural consultant, analyzed Jack Welch's use of hierarchy to drive decisions and behavior in the company.[11] Movement was driven by what Jack Welch valued: speed, flexibility, right actionable decisions, and a business with a commanding position to dominate the market. The organizing principle guided the business strategy: "Be number one or number two in the market for every business, or get out."[12]

A key is how the parts fit together into a comprehensive whole. At GE, under Welch, people at all levels of the organization had a sound basis for making the right actionable decisions and could quickly execute on them. This led to clarity, alignment, right action, and speed.

Welch's message is most compelling because of how it influenced the performance structure. Welch is a master of movement. The decisions he and his executive team made promoted sustained forward movement, even in the face of adversity.

Myopic Vision

Many people are resigned to seeing "present" difficulties as the way things are, without any hope. Why is that? In my opinion, it's because they aren't familiar with the fundamental human capacity to shift their vantage point. They aren't agile in their thought process, and from the perspective that they experience the difficulties, they are right. Managers who don't shift their vantage points won't see an opening for change.

If you want to see the underlying motivating forces, consider doing what great actors do. They act as if the situation is really happening to them. If you were locked out of your house, how would you behave? If you were going to buy new software from a new company, what would you actually be concerned about? Would you intellectualize about being locked out, or would you feel exasperated? Would you conceptualize about the good company that made the product, or would you want to know it's stable and will be around to provide software support? When you want to know what is driving the action, you need to mentally position yourself to have the experience, not fill it in with preconceived notions or biases.

The newly hired executive mentioned earlier in this chapter is representative of our myopic vision. He wasn't living the customer's experience; he was reacting against a preconceived bias of the right culture. In contrast, the VP of Sales had a deep understanding when he answered that "stability" was the critical factor for driving sales.

To Your Success

Have you ever been on a waterslide? Part of the fun is that the waterslide glides you through twisting curves and dumps you into a big pool. How much control do you have? In reality, not much. The waterslide is designed to take you for a ride. You can't get off it in the middle; it guides your movement. At the event level, you just laugh and go with it—you can't do much about it anyway. But if you want to control the experience—and, more particularly, the type of movement—you would change the structures that guide your movement on the slide.

In organizations, you can't always look at the events or the immediate circumstances to determine what is really going on.

We are distracted by the daily circumstances we encounter, and, at minimum, we complain about them. It's not always easy to spot the forces that drive behavior, because we are having so much fun twisting and turning, and then we get dumped into a big pool.

When you see things from the Movement Advantage Point, your explanation for how to create forward movement shifts. It shifts from low-leverage, tactical solutions to high-leverage, strategic solutions. It shifts from using short-term, reactive approaches to establishing a powerful foundation to respond effectively to challenges. It shifts from making fixes that become recurrent problems to building momentum that leads to sustainable success.

The Advantage-Maker's Advice

The forces that drive movement might not be visible, but their consequences are undeniable.
Changing the structure changes the behavior.

Tips and Tools for Creating Momentum

1. Remember Churchill's dictum, "First we shape our structures, and then they shape us."
2. Movement is behavior. For a day, experiment with the lens of movement. See what you and others are doing. Stand back far enough, get to a vantage point, and just notice the movement from one place to another.
3. Evaluate your performance structure. Do unintended competing objectives exist?
4. Can decisions be made clearly, and are resources allocated to those decisions?
5. If your organization isn't aligned, you are probably competing against yourself and not advancing.
6. When push comes to shove, have a hierarchy established that tells people what to include and what to exclude. Establish a "this, not that" policy.
7. Movement is behavior, and you can orchestrate it at the structural force level.

Chapter Recap

1. Movement is behavior. You are at point A, and you want to get results at point B. This approach produces a commanding vantage point to see your best choices.

2. Leadership in its simplest formulation is recognizing your organization's current reality at A, while at the same time knowing where you want to get to, foreseeing what results you will have created at point B, and then mobilizing the forces to move from A to B.

3. Organizations create and have motivating forces that act with and upon them. These invisible powerful forces are similar to the hidden ocean currents that drive the tides.

4. Mishandling the structural forces at play can produce problems. Competing objectives are potential structural conflicts. Before you think an interpersonal conflict exists, check to see if underlying structural forces are causing conflict. Resolving the conflict advances the organization.

5. Just as a riverbed determines a river's course of action, your business has an underlying structure that determines your organization's course of action. Change the structure, and you change the behavior. Establishing a hierarchy of importance lets you know what to do and shifts the odds in your favor.

6. Sometimes managers become so much a part of the culture that an untrained eye can miss the underlying structural reality you face. Don't be deluded by the hope and the hype. Shifting to the right vantage point educates your eyes.

7. The tendency for conflict avoidance is more than just a personality trait; it is an organizational pitfall. If you don't resolve the structural conflict, problems will develop, fester, and deplete the organization.

Endnotes

1. James C. Humes, *The Wit and Wisdom of Winston Churchill: A Treasury of More Than 1,000 Quotations and Anecdotes* (New York: HarperCollins Publishers, 1994).

2. Robert Fritz, *The Path of Least Resistance for Managers* (San Francisco: Berrett-Koehler Publishers, 1999).

3. Frank Lloyd Wright, www.livescience.com/othernews/051129_form_function.html.

4. Robert Fritz, *The Path of Least Resistance for Managers* (San Francisco: Berrett-Koehler Publishers, 1999).

5. *Ibid.*

6. *Ibid.*

7. Jeff Arnold, certified structural consultant, collaborative conversation during consulting project, 2002.

8. Steve Andreas, *Six Blind Elephants: Understanding Ourselves and Each Other* Vol. 1 *Fundamental Principles of Scope and Category* (Moab, UT: Real People Press, 2006).

9. Robert Fritz, *The Path of Least Resistance for Managers* (San Francisco: Berrett-Koehler Publisher, 1999).

10. Alfred Chandler, *Strategy and Structure* (Cambridge, MA: MIT Press, 1962).

11. Mike Scott, certified structural consultant, collaborative conversation regarding Jack Welch, 2002.

12. Robert Slater, *Get Better or Get Beaten: 31 Leadership Secrets from GE's Jack Welch* (New York: Irwin Publishers, 1994).

CHAPTER 8

Strategic Influence: How to Get People to Say Yes in the Right Way to the Right Things

There is no invariable strategic advantage, no invariable position, which can be relied upon at all times.
—Sun Tzu

John F. Kennedy's influence prevented a war with the Soviet Union during the Cuban missile crisis, saving the world from a thermonuclear disaster. In its darkest time, Churchill's influence brought his nation to its finest hour against Nazi Germany. Gandhi's influence liberated the nation of India. Susan B. Anthony's influence in the suffragist movement gave American women the right to vote. Anne Sullivan's influence engaged Helen Keller to become a remarkable and inspiring human being. Kavita Ramdas's influence as the CEO of Global Fund for Women helps the poorest women start businesses, creating transformational social change at the micro level.

Leaders are influencers. At critical moments, they influence. If you are not influencing, it's difficult to think of yourself, or for anyone else to think of you, as a leader. As influential leaders, Advantage-Makers know that there is no time like the present to create the future.

Movers and shakers are influencers of nations, cultures, governments, communities, businesses, organizations, teams, and one-on-one conversations. Recognizing that leadership and influence go hand in hand is immediately graspable. Less obvious is recognizing the advantage-making opportunity—the multiplier effect that results from strategic influence.

The Fourth Advantage Point: Strategic Influence—The Multiplier Effect

Small influential moves can create big leverage gains.

In this chapter and in Chapter 9, "Influence Perception: Helping People See What They Need to See," we focus on eight influence factors to help identify opportunities to influence perception. As an advantage-making leader, you shift the odds in your favor through strategic influence. Timing is important in taking advantage of and creating influence.

At a conference titled "Leadership in an Era of Uncertainty and Change," former Enron Vice President and whistleblower Sherron Watkins said that before the collapse of the enterprise, she had approached the CEO of Enron, Ken Lay, about problems with the firm's accounting practices. "I thought I was handing Ken Lay his 'leadership moment,' but he chose not to seize it."[1]

Carpe Influence

My Dad knew what to say, when to say it, and how to say it to get somebody to do something. Most people perceived him as a master of influence. Never formally going to college, he only took a few night classes. In fact, he never officially graduated from high school. My grandparents put him to work helping the family make ends meet. Although he did what had to be done, my Dad would've preferred to have completed high school and college. While he didn't have academic training, he was street-smart. He was beyond street-smart; he was streetwise. His influence skills grew from negotiating on New York City's streets. "You learn fast when you're hungry," he impressed upon me. I was fortunate to sit at the feet of the master. I was especially fortunate because he loved me and fed me. But sometimes he let me go a little hungry. He was an entrepreneur before the word became popular. He could speak and connect with people on the streets of New York, Main Street, or Wall Street.

Knowing what to say is essential, but what distinguishes great influencers is that they know when to say it. Timing is critical. *Carpe* influence: Seize the influence moment. Skilled influencers are in sync with the moment. When the opportunity to influence arises, you need to seize it. Advantage-Makers create the opportune time with their influence. My Dad had a great secret sauce. His timing was impeccable. Time and again, he turned the tables from defeat to victory. He had his defeats, but they didn't keep him down for long.

Why didn't his defeats keep him down? He was hungry and wanted things to be better—this promoted his resilience. His great sense of timing enabled him to see that things were not permanent and defeats were only temporary. And finally, he knew how to influence others; this bolstered his confidence to advance forward.

Unbeknownst to him, some of his secret sauce was actually codified in the academic world of social psychology and, in particular, social influence. This chapter translates those findings into strategic influence for advantage-making leaders.

Strategic influence is a key Advantage-Maker tool because it increases your ability to recognize unexpected opportunities and persuade others without relying on coercion.

1. Framing Relevant Self-Interest

The first factor of influence involves penetrating to the heart of the matter—relevant self-interest. This skill was an essential part of the secret sauce; if you couldn't do that, you were an also-ran. You need to touch the special places in people. You need to know what makes them tick emotionally. What is their pain? What do they want to gain? People are preoccupied with their own problems. In other words, my Dad tracked their self-interest, enlightened or otherwise.

Your brain is hardwired for survival. You are constantly managing your preservation, balancing what needs to be maintained with what needs to be adjusted to continue surviving. In their book *Selling to the Old Brain,* Christophe Morin and Patrick Renvoise reveal how new discoveries in brain research can be applied to influence.[2] The main premise is that the final decision maker rests in what they refer to as the "Old Brain" center. The Old Brain's function is self-preservation—me, me, me. The classic question "What's in it for me?" requires answers even for the most altruistic of us. Individuals are self-organizing around what matters to them—their preservation and their opportunities.

Advantage-Makers shift their focus until they hit upon the relevant leverage that makes a difference to the Old Brain, in Morin and Renvoise's terms. To do this, you need a vantage point.

Can you grasp the real story? Too often we miss what people are really telling us. You need to listen to the narrative for what's really at stake. Listening to others' struggles, my Dad recognized their hopes and desires, what they were really after, and what they were dodging, denying, or distorting. His radar was acute; sensing their fears, he could see the obstacles in front of them. Is your radar working? Are you paying attention to yourself or to others? If you are paying attention to yourself, your radar might not provide you with clear signals. As an Advantage-Maker, you want to recognize how others' attempts failed and what might instead succeed.

Vivid Gain or Pain

Can relevant self-interest be influenced? When things are relevant, they are related, significant, and applicable to us.

If something is not pertinent or is unrelated to us, we are not interested in it. In the midst of continuous attempts to grab our attention, relevance is triggered by what is most vivid to us. Research suggests that vivid information is more influential. Vivid information attracts our attention; our self-preservation survival radar identifies gain or pain. You don't need to convince people to own the action if they see it as personally relevant.

Our names are vivid for us. If I say "Terri," and this is your name, you will shift your attention to what I'm saying.

Headlines are presented in vivid ways. There is a news channel just for headline news. Which of the following statements do you want to know more about?

- A fact about a lost wallet
- A winning lottery ticket found in a lost wallet

The second statement engages us. In any presentation, you want to make sure your headlines are vivid. A picture is worth a thousand words, and that phrase is worth a thousand pictures. Influential people do not lull you to sleep, nor do they dull you to tears.

When thinking about buying a particular car, you begin to notice more of them. They've always been there, but now your relevant self-interest becomes vividly aware of them.

Managers organize around vividly framed objectives, opportunities, and rewards. Potential failure is riveting. They pay relatively little attention to activities outside their area of focus. Saying they are generally preoccupied with their own problems is an understatement. When they walk into a meeting, each manager has their own personal agenda. When agendas coincide, mutual self-interest exists; when the agendas don't overlap, the managers each return to their own agenda. And then the fun begins.

Vivid Framing

Most arguments are won or lost by virtue of how the issue is framed. Would you eat meat that had 15% fat? Wouldn't it feel healthier if it were 85% lean? It's the same meat, yet framed differently and perceived differently. Mouthwash is mouthwash. Take Listerine—it kills germs. That's a fact—no frame there, right? Well, along comes Scope, and they frame the argument around being good-tasting versus causing medicine breath. The results taste better to Scope, because it wins a piece of market share.

Vivid framing directs our attention; the frame acts as a lens to interpret the facts. Frame the issue and make it vivid. The most compelling frame wins, no matter what the facts are.

During budgetary meetings, the CEO asks for budgets from each department head. He or she then requests input on different allocation decisions, such as research and development, training and development, and head count. As expected, each department head argues that his or her needs are primary and that more funds should be allocated to his or her function. Is this just a selfish, self-serving conclusion? Sometimes. However, there's another dimension to this behavior. Max Bazerman offers a different explanation: although it's still relevant self-interest, it's because each person's needs are most vivid to him or her.[3] Let me say it another way: what stands out is what is most vivid, and what is most vivid stands out. Getting back to the CEO's allocation decision, who or what wins? Whatever is most vivid to the CEO.

Researchers Brad Bell and Elizabeth Loftus have found that case studies are more memorable because they are more vivid than statistical facts.[4] If you're building an argument and want it to be memorable, present a vivid case study representative of your point.

If you want your valid arguments to be valued, make them vivid.

An extremely bright and talented executive made valid but not vivid arguments. He was ignored and believed inconsequential. In effect, he bungled his opportunity to persuade. His valid information was overlooked in favor of information presented vividly. When he learned to make his valid ideas vivid, he became more influential. To influence others, you must speak to relevant self-interests, gains, or pains that are vividly depicted.

2. Reciprocity: Give a Little, Get a Lot

Do you want to know why people do what they do? As a street psychologist, my Dad had strong insight into what made people tick. He watched. He figured. He laughed. He had a great sense of humor and made people laugh. Comedians know what people are thinking better than psychologists do. At one time, my Dad owned an Italian restaurant and pizzeria in New York City. (It wasn't called Feinberg's Pizza, although our family knows how to make great pizza.) At the restaurant, we had three chefs. One chef was a compulsive gambler, always betting and listening to the horse races on the radio while cooking. A second chef imagined himself a Hungarian hit man—yet he was afraid of his own shadow, drank a lot, and was actually quite considerate. The third chef literally escaped from a mental institution. And you think you have difficult people at work. They were the salt and pepper of the earth. You can imagine your own stories with this crew—multiply it by ten, and you know the reality of that work environment.

In the midst of these cuckoo workers, my Dad made the business work. He took a little hole-in-the-wall pizza business that had only takeout and delivery service—there wasn't anyplace to sit down—and made it sing.

To give you a picture of the neighborhood, 600 families lived in just the two apartment buildings closest to the restaurant. Dozens of other apartment buildings were within short driving distance. When my Dad took over the business, he had my cousin Deanna, a TV ad copywriter, pen some copy about the new restaurant and how his ownership would make the food better. He had 20 years of experience in the meat business, was finicky about what he ate, and wouldn't send out anything that wasn't equal to the quality that he demanded for himself. To increase business, he had the local kids distribute the flyers and menus in exchange for 10 dollars, a meal, and all the dessert they wanted—Italian ices. The flyers produced a healthy uptick in business.

A month later, he used the same flyer and had the kids distribute it again. But this time, he attached a dime to each one with a message that said, "Make the call on us." Phone calls were only ten cents at this time. How did the dime tactic affect business? Well, the phone didn't stop ringing. We had three order takers and five delivery drivers; each driver carried five meals per trip. (By the way, my Dad invented hot boxes before they became popular—he could have made a mint just producing those boxes.) The drivers were running in and out of the restaurant, going as fast as they could, and the phones were still ringing at midnight when we shut the doors. Although the three chefs were "nuts," they were incredibly good producers. The financial results were several orders of magnitude above what we had ever taken in before. Can this tactic be applied to managers and their organizations?

Do unto Others...

For a dime, people just couldn't pass this up. What was going on here? What a tremendous return on investment (ROI). Small move, big payoff—clearly, a multiplier effect. I later learned more about this phenomenon and how to replicate it from another master of influence. I started with the practical master of influence and went to the professor who wrote the book on influence, revealing the factors that all of us can reproduce and use. Dr. Robert Cialdini, a distinguished Regent's professor at Arizona State University and past President of the Society of Personality and Social Psychology, wrote *Influence: Science and Practice*, a best seller that has sold more than a million copies.

When I spoke with Bob Cialdini about the "ten cents—make the call on us" strategy, he identified my father's instinctive code as employing the principle of reciprocity.[5] This principle is the basis of mutual exchange in society. In popular language, "What goes around, comes around." In its application, the rule to follow is, before you make a request or want something, give something. The impact of reciprocity has been quantified for a variety of situations. At each venue, whether it involves international negotiations, donations to the Veteran's Administration, tips in the service industry, or closing sales, the implementer of reciprocity has realized a marked increase in agreement and reward.[6]

The emphasis is on relationships, not disingenuous manipulation of people. It's a natural ethic of doing what's right—a value structure that springs from a generosity of spirit, a natural give-and-take. Skilled influencers want both sides to win.

The reciprocity principle for my Dad would simply be, "You give to get." Make it easy and desirable for customers to do business with you. Give them a dime, and they will be inclined to take you up on your offer. In management roles, many managers take the opposite approach. They need to be given something before they are willing to reciprocate. Some are still waiting and wondering why people seldom support their requests. A number of my clients have been surprised to find that initiating—being first to do unto others what you would want done unto you—changes the interaction and shifts the odds to getting what they want.

Increasing Your Social Capital

At the University of San Francisco in the Department of Organizational Studies, I teach a course entitled "Social and Organization Networks." The core of the course focuses on social capital. In business, we have financial, physical, and social capital. Social capital is about relationships and their natural benefits. This is the glue in making organizations work; it's part of the informal underlying structure that produces results. In the midst of great change, it's a reliable factor that you can call upon to make things work that shouldn't. When you can't get things done through formal channels, the skilled Advantage-Maker uses the social capital channel.

Central to all marketing is winning the hearts and minds of your customers—that is, establishing relationships that create loyal, returning customers. Nordstrom's brand, for example, is known for creating social capital and building enduring customer relationships and evangelical word-of-mouth marketing.

Executives not only market their products to customers, but they also market themselves internally. Social capital expands the pie inside the organization. If you have this social capital skill, it increases the demand for your talent and contribution.

Don't underestimate the social capital channel. Respecting others, doing favors, and helping others feels good, increases the likelihood that they will reciprocate in kind. People like to return the favor. Harvey Mackay's book *Dig Your Well Before*

You're Thirsty demonstrates the power of social networks.[7] People helping people is fast, efficient, and relatively inexpensive. And it makes you feel good, according to brain research. Doing things for others actually creates a neurochemical process that boosts our happiness.[8]

Bungling Social Capital

Unfortunately, social capital, typically referred to as people skills and organizational savvy, is often bungled. Bungling social capital is bungling organizational effectiveness, and it reflects on leaders. Recall the CEO in an earlier chapter who said "My business is business; my business is not communication." Although he's technically correct, operationally he was deficient, and it cost him millions of dollars in business. He bungled both money and opportunity.

The second influence factor, then, is the social capital generated by reciprocity. Reciprocity can be readily applied in your leadership endeavors to create advantages.

When I was a teenager, my Dad and I had a disagreement about how to get ahead, how to get what you want. In one of our classic "teen battles," he reminded me that it's who you know that matters. In true adolescent fashion (my adolescence lasted into my early 30s), I said it was what you know that matters. In effect, the difference of opinion was the "who you know" versus "what you know" question. Social networks are a source of social capital because they embrace both the relationships and the value of the content to others.

Detecting Influence

The influence factors are powerful; they are overlooked by some and misused by others. Central to Cialdini's work is ethical social influence. He refers to an ethical influence agent as someone who imports the influence principle into situations that naturally warrant it. Ethical influence agents search for the situation's naturally occurring aspect to apply their influence. No more, no less. If you illicitly import an influence principle, manipulating falsehoods, you are misusing influence. However, more ethical-influence opportunities exist than most people realize.

There are detectors of influence, misusers of influence, and bunglers of influence. Cialdini, who coined the term "bunglers of influence," thinks of bunglers of influence as well-intended people who might not know the principles.[9] They might think there is something wrong with influencing, or they might not know how to detect or use the principles skillfully.

At a program on strategic influence, executives, salespeople, and negotiators realized they weren't detecting or using the influence principles and had missed opportunities that were right in front of them. All were surprised at the extent to which they had inadvertently bungled opportunities both inside the organization and outside with customers. For them, becoming consciously competent of the nuances of influence was similar to finding the mother lode of advantage-making. What was really unexpected and amazing is that these people were not novices; they were experienced, accomplished performers, tops in their respective fields.

Recognizing and Using Reciprocity

In one of my first consulting assignments, an executive team was in the midst of a dysfunctional conflict. We met on Friday, but the issue wasn't resolved. I offered to meet the next day. The CEO looked at me in amazement and said, "You'll meet with us on Saturday?" "I think this topic is really important and want to get us moving in the right direction," I replied. We met and resolved the conflict. Later, the CEO commented that he had made a good decision in hiring me because I was willing to work on the weekend. People appreciate that little extra; they realize you're looking out for their best interests.

When the CEO was surprised at my offer to work on Saturday, I could have said "No problem." Many well-intended people habitually bungle these moments. Had I only said "No problem," the CEO would have turned his attention to the difficulty they were confronting. Is that bad? No; it simply misses an opportunity to solidify the relationship.[10] I was ready, able, and willing to provide the help they needed. This was, in fact, service beyond the contract. I honestly cared about helping them and doing it in a timely manner. You can undervalue the social capital being developed if you only think "I am just doing my job" when in fact you are making a big effort that matters. Making the effort and conveying it in a respectful way—they have a real problem; let's resolve it and move in the right direction—will strengthen your future of working together. I've worked with this leader for a long time, and it's been my pleasure.

In business, do your customers feel they are getting special or unique treatment? If they don't, you have an opportunity to take action and establish a stronger sense of loyalty. When we give a little something extra, we solidify the relationship. In some situations, you might simply need to provide a "gesture of giving" to the other party.

Do you first give and then make your requests?

One of the simplest and most well-received gifts you can offer is your positive attention. Find something you like about the person. In difficult negotiations, appreciate something about your counterpart; it can reduce the time to agreement significantly, as well as the wrangling.

Appreciation was my mom's influence secret; she was the one who actually made everything work with all the difficult personalities in the restaurant. She would ignore most of what she didn't like and warmly comment on what she did. She gave each of us gifts that we didn't receive anywhere else. In return, people did things for her that no one else could get them to do. When people know you like them, they think that you have their best interests at heart and will look out for them.

Strategic Retreat

What do you do when a person rejects your influence request? Many influence agents give a concession. And with the concession, the person returns the favor. Fund-raising campaigns employ this strategy. Once you have agreed that it is a good cause (and that's critical), they ask you for money—let's say, $100. You reply that the amount is too much. They move to a concession and ask for $25. You pause and then return the favor—you agree. Instead of betting everything on one "yes," the gambit is to have a natural retreat to something you will say yes to. This fallback position is something you wanted. And besides, $25 is a small amount compared to $100. We will see how this comparison is also part of the strategic influence process at work.

Preparing strategic retreats in advance of your request can create wins where defeat would have seemed inevitable. People are always free to decline or have their own reasons for rejection. Your requests can be seen in an even stronger light when you are a credible source, which is our next influence factor.

3. Source Credibility: Trustworthiness Plus Competence

My family's dinner table was similar to those of most families. Whenever someone had a strong position, there would be questions. Although they were often funny, they typically led to checking the source of information. How reliable was that person? Invariably, my Dad described the motivation and, at times, people's biases—what they were up to, what they were for or against, why they said what they did, and what was in it for them to do what they were doing. The message clearly was, "Check your sources and their biases." Whenever you get advice, it might be inadequate, if not altogether wrong.

The third influence factor is source credibility. Credible sources are particularly influential for decision makers; they are believable. The simple rule we all follow is, "Let's do what the expert says." This simple rule saves time. Authorities must know what they are doing, so just follow their lead.

Are You an Expert?

Who gets to be considered an expert? Round up the usual suspects—people with credentials, titles, and positions. Two elements establish the communicator's source credibility: trustworthiness and competence. Someone can be trustworthy but not competent. Another could be competent but not trustworthy. In both cases his or her credibility is suspect. As a legitimate authority you are a credible source, and your influence is immediate when you speak.

If you succeed in your job, you get to write the story and increase your stock as an expert. History, after all, is written by the winners. In the book *The 22 Immutable Laws of Marketing*, Jack Trout and Al Ries suggest that an expert is someone who is perceived to be an expert.[11] By whom? By the person doing the perceiving.

According to R. Petty and J. Cacioppo, people are "motivated to hold correct attitudes."[12] Your argument can encounter an obstacle—that is, what people think is the correct attitude on the issue. Their attitudes can be more or less malleable. In part, this depends on the extent to which the audience thinks about your argument. Imagine a continuum: On one end, little thinking occurs about the issues; on the other end, a great deal of thought occurs. If the members of the audience believe themselves to be experts, they won't be easily persuaded to a different way of thinking. They must recognize your expertise on the topic, and your arguments need to be stronger and qualitatively better. The good news is, once they change their mind, it will persist.

When the audience or target for your influence doesn't have strong opinions, or if they don't already know a lot about the topic, bringing your expertise or the credibility of other sources to bear can be persuasive in getting quick agreement. In other words, people tend to rely on the expert—knowing that the source is the doctor, scientist, technical whiz, organizational leader, and so on.

Make Your Leadership Distinctive

Generally, we hire managers who are knowledgeable about their industry. The more expert they are and the more authoritatively they speak, the greater our confidence is in their opinions and abilities. When someone moves from the category of "they know something" to the "rank of authority," we not only view them differently, but they also affect us differently. Authority might be based upon position or know-how. Most of us are aware of the influence of authority, but not to the actual extent. When the buzz within the organization is that you are an expert, you gain a seat at the "influence table."

Leadership is a credential. Distinguishing yourself as an Advantage-Maker further differentiates you. It can become your brand, what you are known for, just as Coke is known as the leading cola and Xerox as the leading copier. What makes you unique and puts you in the mind of the organization as an Advantage-Maker? Your advantage-making can be as a team player, people person, strategic thinker, transformational expert, turnaround specialist, thought leader, or business negotiator. Herb Kelleher, former CEO of Southwest Airlines and an Advantage-Maker, was clearly the inspiration for Southwest's culture and humorous style, as well as the impetus behind Southwest's awards for being the most admired and most profitable airline.

Expertise is critical for managerial success. We defer to experts. The danger is we can use the expert rule, the heuristics of expertise, too quickly, reducing our thinking and, subsequently, the outcomes. For example, a number of accomplished executives have been turned down for positions because they didn't have industry expertise. Although knowing your industry is beneficial, sometimes industry expertise is inappropriate as the sole criteria for evaluating future performance. The same holds true for deciding whether you should look inside the company or go outside to fill a managerial vacancy. We become blinded by familiarity, as the Laws of Defeat reveal. In the right situation, outside managers can see things that have become too familiar for insiders to see. In turning around an ailing IBM, outsider CEO Lou Gerstner demonstrated his managerial prowess and influence, in spite of not having industry- or company-specific expertise.

Although expertise and authority are on the royal road to influence, for some audiences, disagreeing with an authority or expert is a pastime. Followers really notice and appreciate leaders who judiciously use their power.

Counterintuitive Strategies to Enhance Credibility

Most leaders know that credibility is critical to their effectiveness and influence in the organization. Without credibility, you won't be trusted. What might not be as obvious is how to develop trust with new groups of strangers. Lawyers, for example, influence groups of strangers to agree with the case they are advocating.

A jury was listening as the defense attorney began his summation: "You might not like my style; I'm a bit brusque. I realize it. My wife is trying to help me out on that. I tell you this only so that you don't hold it against my client." The jury nodded. He then went on to tell the jury that his client was a good man, but he had his faults and made mistakes as well; he wasn't perfect. Again the jury nodded. At that point the attorney changed his approach and presented the facts that proved his client's innocence. What was the lawyer doing? His arguments began with weaknesses and then switched. If we were on the jury, we would have believed the weaknesses; he was now credible. Then the jury listened as the frame of a truth-sayer took hold and the facts became evident. The man was found innocent. By first arguing against themselves, credible influencers know that their audience will tend to believe the next thing they say. It disarms the listener. Arguing against your interests is not saying you are incompetent. You become an honest broker of information. Paradoxically, you strengthen your source of credibility. You can move an audience from polite and skeptical to engaged and appreciative.

Alice Eagly and colleagues found that subjects displayed greater attitude change when they believed the communicator had taken a position that did not reflect bias.[13] People tend to think that speakers try to say what will please their audience. When speakers don't tell the audience what they expect to hear, the audience sees them as less biased. Furthermore, when speakers don't say things that fit their background (gender, ethnicity, and age), the audience sees them as less biased. The incongruity with expectations makes their words compelling, if not convincing.

Arguing against an aspect of your case is a proven influence strategy in the world of marketing. Consider L'Oreal's slogan of "Expensive but you're worth it," or Listerine's slogan of "the taste you hate, twice a day." Consumers agree they are expensive and distasteful, respectively. After Grape-Nuts launched its slogan of "a learned pleasure; try it for a week," sales rose 23%. The purpose of the candor isn't to drive people away, and it isn't a *mea culpa;* instead, it establishes a convincing relationship.

In your one-on-one leadership conversations, team meetings, and presentations, do you try to make things look rosy and perfect when they aren't?

It's a mistake to approach things this way if known problems exist. People can see through you as if you're made of Swiss cheese. You lose credibility. Yet I've witnessed executives pretending that the difficulties in the argument didn't exist. They enter board meetings putting on their best face, and their presentation is attacked. Compare that to executives who present the facts—the good, the bad, and the ugly—and then provide a "get well" strategy. We tend to believe that these presenters have a grasp on reality and can do something positive about it.

This issue illustrates one of the most important questions about how to influence ethically. Should you tell people about a weakness in your argument? If you don't, you will be dodging the entire time. Your credibility will be questioned, and once that happens, the rest of what you say will rapidly diminish in value to the audience.

But when do you tell them? Early or later, after you've warmed them up? The answer appears to be early on—maybe not the first thing, but soon enough that you can dispense with the "gotcha" group.

In difficult situations, executives fail when they don't appropriately argue, at least moderately, against themselves. They are spin doctors whose spin we don't believe. We see them as biased, and we hold it against them. We conclude that they don't have our best interests at heart.

This strategy of moderately arguing against yourself is counterintuitive. Yet it is consistent with the Game-Changer approach (see Chapter 6, "The Game Changer: If You Are in a Hole, Stop Digging and Change the Game"). At the same time, it values truth and reality. The second-order change approach takes us out of the usual system and goes to another level where the problem doesn't exist. How do we reduce a credibility problem? Argue both for and against our view. We are perceived as unbiased agents of influence, telling the truth and demonstrating that we are in touch with reality.

This paradoxical strategy demonstrates our authority, expertise, and credibility. Showing the weakness in our argument early on strengthens our arguments. In a confrontational situation, we take the wind out of our opponent's sails by playing mental judo and neutralizing the adversary's attack points. In a collaborative business exchange, we are seen as looking after not only our own interests, but also the interests of the other party. We can be frank with each other and find solutions together.

Other People Can Enhance Your Credibility

A testimonial by an authority figure is a shortcut to believability. Having an endorsement by a reputable expert brings a cache that turns prospects into customers. By virtue of the testimonial, we are willing to grant credence to the claims and move closer to agreeing to the request.

These behaviors are common. What's unusual is the extent to which we are biased—automatically accepting an expert's opinion instead of our rational thought process. Douglas Peters and Steven Ceci demonstrated this bias in their study on article selection for scholarly journals.[14] Twelve articles that had been previously published in journals by authors from prestigious universities were resubmitted. However, this time the names and affiliations of the authors were changed to unknown authors from a modest human-potential center. The results revealed that eight of the nine resubmitted articles that had previously been accepted were now rejected. (Three of the articles were detected and recognized as prior submissions.) Nothing changed in the papers except the writers' credentials. The counterfeit authors had lost their pedigree, and, with that, their words lost their luster.

These curious findings have implications for Advantage-Makers. First, they confirm the power of being perceived as an authority. Second, they reveal how little we actually recognize the effects of a "lack of authority" on our judgment. Third, they require us to reconsider the factors we include to make requests. If you are not, getting agreement, you may be underestimating your audience's need for credible sources. During the ceremony for completing my master's degree at Tulane University, I promised myself I would never go back to school. I was done. I had just graduated and walked up the aisle after the ceremonies were complete. At the end of the aisle, my Dad reached out, shook my hand, and congratulated me. It was a great moment. It was a great moment for influence. In his next breath, he said, "What's this I hear that you could do better in life if you had a PhD?" He understood the value of a credential and its impact on others. His translation: PhD=doors open.

In the next section, we look at the impact of people who are similar to us.

4. Source Similarity: Finding Common Ground

The refrain "People are the most important asset" can actually be realized from a social influence perspective. A fourth source of influence is social validation—what people who are similar to us think. When employed skillfully, you can legitimately align people on difficult decisions through source similarity.

Leon Festinger found that people take their cues from others who are similar.[15] We tend to be creatures of social comparison; by comparing our views with others, we validate our view—*especially in times of uncertainty*. Source similarity is noticing what people who are similar to us are thinking and doing, to confirm what is correct.

Birds of a feather flock together. Peer-group pressure. People behave based upon how they perceive others behaving. Similar people think alike and engage in similar activities. The features that tend to be most significant are similar attitudes ("She thinks like I do").[16] Winning the hearts and minds of your audience by demonstrating commonalities can lead to behavior change.

However, the similarity must be relevant to the issue being decided—apples to apples, not apples to spinach. A technology executive talking to engineers about the future of the technology industry has more influence in that arena than when giving his or her opinion on who will win the World Series.

Using Similarity to Influence

How can leaders use this source similarity knowledge? Change programs and new initiatives require leadership influence. If you, as the leader, have encountered resistance, you might try to dissuade people from their ideas. Sometimes your authority will suffice. You might have many one-on-one meetings. Although connecting with employees is important, the size of your organization can limit the contact.

In keeping with the Advantage-Maker's performance theme to get more out of every resource, you should identify key influencers or pockets of influence within the group—people who others identify with and typically follow.

Discuss the issue with trusted key influencers; by gaining their endorsement, you bring along the entire group. Specifically, ask them to speak, either informally or formally, to the rest of the team and, at key moments, stand up for the initiative. Strategically orchestrate the change instead of overpowering team members.

A director of engineering wanted a proposal to develop from within his engineering team instead of forcing it on them from on high. Without any fanfare and capturing an opportune moment, he privately asked one of the senior managers what he thought should be done. It was consistent with the director's idea. He then asked the senior manager if he would circulate his thinking before the next staff meeting. The senior manager appreciated the opportunity to contribute. Many such opportunities exist.

When is IBM not a good role model? Most of us are aware of the IBM salesperson method stating, "No one ever got fired for buying IBM." In other words, everyone (social proof) buys IBM. Although IBM is a great reference account for credibility, it might not seal the deal, because most companies are not similar enough to IBM.

Most start-up firms work hard to acquire referenceable accounts. In persuading new prospects to buy their products, they should make sure that their prospects can identify with (be similar to) the accounts they reference. A hidden resistance often goes unspoken if you try to present a great argument but it doesn't match the prospect's internal question. The prospect is usually thinking, "Their product sounds good, but the examples they are using aren't similar to me. Will this work in my business?" The remedy is to find a match between the prospect and your references. The decision moment arises when you provide references. The closer the match, the more influence you achieve.

Community of Users

Establishing networks or a community of users is another way to employ similarity in business. The community of users is a network that spreads the word rapidly. Product launches that deploy social proof—other people talking—typically are more successful and quicker than those that don't. When a community (such as Mac users) begins to realize that many of its members are using a particular product, this boosts sales rapidly. Winning the hearts and minds of a community is a powerful asset. If other people we like, admire, and respect welcome a new recommendation, we probably should as well.

Further examples of social proof are the *New York Times* best sellers list, anything rated number one by users, top ten business schools, best-places-to-eat polls, favorite magazines for car buyers, and so on.

Social comparison—taking cues from those who are similar—is a powerful tool for leaders. We relate well to people who think, feel, and act similar to us; these are typically people we trust. They provide us clues for the right direction. You use social comparisons when you wonder what your coworkers and colleagues think about a particular issue.

Let others speak for you, on your behalf. You've been influenced by this strategy a thousand times. If you have a backache, who do you go to? To the chiropractor that a friend of yours went to? We do business with businesses that are endorsed by people we like, admire, and respect.

Notice the difference between these:

1. Try my service for xyz benefits.
2. Try my service—100 people similar to you have received xyz benefit.

This one small change can have a huge impact on your requests and your advantage-making ability. The way you say something makes a difference.

Leaders Who Stray from the Common Ground

Unfortunately, some managers refuse to employ social similarity. These are the do-it-yourself managers. Two types of do-it-yourself managers exist: those who are committed to doing it themselves and those who don't realize they are missing an opportunity.

Typically, committed do-it-yourself managers are no-nonsense task drivers who might be overly controlling; they try to show how influential they can be. They will change people's minds and convince them on whatever topic is at hand. Their attitude is "Let me talk to them; people will do what I ask." Sometimes this works. As we've seen, authority and expertise can be very convincing—at times, mindlessly convincing.

If you are an inadvertent do-it-yourself manager, it behooves you to shift and employ the help of others when appropriate. When your own authority doesn't carry sufficient credibility on a specific task, it is useful to ask people who are similar to those you are trying to persuade to deliver the message.

Leading to "Yes"

We've reviewed four powerful influencers:

1. Vivid framing of relevant arguments
2. Reciprocity designed to give first and then receive
3. Source credibility that demonstrates your lack of bias
4. Source similarity to show social proof

In the next chapter, we continue discussing how to influence perceptions, focusing on how to establish a favorable psychological environment that will naturally increase the likelihood of people saying yes to your request.

Note

Chapters 8 and 9 both cover strategic influence and are recapped together at the end of Chapter 9.

Endnotes

1. Sherron Watkins, *Power Failure: The Inside Story of How Enron's Culture of Arrogance and Greed Led to the Biggest Bankruptcy in American History* (Random House, 2003).

2. Patrick Renvoise and Christophe Morin, *Selling to the Old Brain* (CA: Salesbrain, 2002).

3. Max Bazerman, "Negotiation Online," Harvard Business School Newsletter (2004).

4. Brad Bell and Elizabeth Loftus, "Vivid persuasion in the courtroom," *Journal of Personality Assessment*, 49, 659–664, 1985. Appeared in *Dynamics of Persuasion* (Hillsdale, N.J.: Lawrence Erlbaum Associates, 1993).

5. Robert Cialdini, in personal communication, 2005.

6. Robert Cialdini, *Influence: Science and Practice*, 4th ed. (Needham Heights, MA: Allyn & Bacon, 2001).

7. Harvey Mackay, *Dig Your Well Before You're Thirsty* (New York: A Currency Book, 1997).

8. Sonja Lyubomirsky, Kennon Sheldon, David Schkade, "Pursuing happiness: The architecture of sustainable change," *Review of General Psychology*, 2005 – 138.23.71.114.

    J. Rilling, D. Gutman, T. Zeh, G. Pagnoni, G. Berns, C.Kilts, "A neural basis for social cooperation," *Neuron*, 2002 Jul 18; 35(2): 395–405.

    E. Fehr, B. Rockenbach, "Human altruism: economic, neural, and evolutionary perspectives," *Curr Opin Neurobiol*, 2004 Dec; 14(6): 784–90.

9. Robert Cialdini, "Principles of Persuasion" course, Arizona State University, 2003.

10. At Cialdini's "Principles of Persuasion" workshop, I discovered I was already avoiding a serious bungling of influence—the "no problem" communication tendency was problematic.

11. Jack Trout and Al Ries, *The 22 Immutable Laws of Marketing* (New York: HarperBusinss, 1993).

12. R. Petty and J. Cacioppo, *Communications and Persuasion: Central and Peripheral Routes to Attitude Change* (New York: Springer-Verlag, 1986).

13. Alice Eagly, W. Wood, and S. Chaiken, "Causal inferences about communicators and their effect on opinion change." *Journal of Personality and Social Psychology*, 36, 424–435, 1978. Appeared in *Influence: Science and Practice*, 4th ed. (Needham Heights, MA: Allyn & Bacon, 2001).

14. Douglas Peters and Steven Ceci, "Peer-review practices of the psychological journals: The fate of published articles," *The Behavioral and Brain Sciences*, 5, 187–195, 1982. Appeared in *Influence: Science and Practice*, 4th ed. (Needham Heights, MA: Allyn & Bacon, 2001).

15. Leon Festinger, "A Theory of Social Comparisons," Human Relations 7 (1954): 117–140.

16. D. J. O'Keefe, *Persuasion: Theory and Research* (Newbury Park, CA: Sage, 1990).

CHAPTER 9

Influence Perception: Helping People See What They Need to See

Carpenters bend wood. Fletchers bend arrows.
Wise men fashion themselves.

—Buddha

5. Brains Like Contrast—And So Should Influencers

Contrasts—your brain likes them. Light and dark. Man and woman. Parent and child. Success and failure. Winners and losers. Leaders and followers. Contrasts create tensions. Contrary to popular opinion, your brain likes tension; it leads to anticipation of its resolution. It's what movies are all about. Protagonist and antagonists. Boy meets girl. Boy loses girl. Girl takes boy back. The tension seeks resolution.[1] Good movies have strong tension. Good leaders establish strong tension in the organization. Good salespeople create strong tension in prospects. Good marketers create strong tension that results in consumer desire. Your brain likes contrast and tension because it creates desire. If you don't have contrast, you don't have tension, desire, and, most important, movement.

If you want to influence people and create movement, become a master of contrasts. The contrast principle establishes the comparison. "Our product is the best." Everyone says that, but if it's not put in the right context, it loses its power to influence. A recent ad distinguished one company compared to the rest: "Other companies save you 50% over ten years; we can save you 50% in two years." This contrast gets people's attention.

The most powerful contrast you can create in marketing is "We are *the only* ones who...." Although many principles of influence exist that you can, and should, learn, the one that underlies every other principle is *contrast.*

Let's consider an example of how to use contrast. Robert Cialdini consulted with a client that manufactured a high-end, deluxe spa for $15,000. It wasn't selling. He suggested the salespeople create a genuine contrast in the minds of their prospects by asking how much it would cost to build an addition onto their house. In that geographical area, the cost was about $75,000. "Well," the salesperson was then instructed to say, "our deluxe spa is like adding on another room. For only $15,000, you can have a beautiful addition in the form of a spa." Did this work? Sales went up 540%![2] The contrast proved influential. The cost of an additional room was compared with the cost of the spa, and this produced the desired contrast effect.

The contrast principle basically involves setting up a psychological environment, a context in which to make a judgment. First you set up a context, and then you make the request. The basic question to ask yourself is, "Compared to what?"

Think "How much would an addition to your house cost?" Then offer the deluxe spa that creates similar results at a much lower price. Such a deal. A concrete context—an addition to your house—establishes a compelling contrast. The additional room also became the anchor point from which to see the deluxe spa. If an additional room in the prospect's neighborhood had cost around $20,000 instead of $75,000, the contrast would not have seemed as compelling.

The real masters of influence always establish the context before they make a request. But it isn't just any context; it's a favorable context. We can change a person's perception and his or her experience by structuring what comes immediately beforehand.

Undergraduate psychology programs typically require students to participate in lab experiments. In one experiment, a professor engaged his students in the following psycho-physiological experiment. Three buckets were placed in front of students. The bucket in the middle had room-temperature water. On either side, one bucket had ice water, and another had hot water. Students placed their hands in each outside bucket—hot and cold. The hand that first experienced the hot water was then placed in the middle bucket, with room-temperature water. The students reported the middle bucket had cold water in it. The hand initially in the ice water was then placed in the middle bucket, with room-temperature water. Surprised, the students blurted out that the bucket had hot water. One hot, one cold. A complete contrast, and nothing had changed; students simply perceived it differently. The middle bucket is what I refer to as the "bucket of perception." Students experienced the bucket of perception differently based upon what came before—the hot or cold water. Technically, this phenomenon is known as the *perceptual contrast.*

Create a "bucket of perception."

Leaders persuade, and if you examine how they persuade, you will notice that the great persuasive leaders employ the contrast principle. "Ask not what your country can do for you; ask what you can do for your country," urged John F. Kennedy.[3] A clear, unexpected contrast. The more unexpected the contrast, the more powerfully it remains with us. Remember, our brains like contrast and tension. Something that is unexpected creates more contrast and, therefore, more tension.

Considering all the models and principles of influence, if I could pick only one, contrast would be it. Contrast becomes the anchor point from which to perceive the offer. What you do before you make your request is most important; it creates an emotional environment in which your listener will consider your offer. Your first step is to contrast and then make a request.

Judgment Depends on Context

People compare contexts and then draw conclusions. Judgment requires a context. Establish a context for your audience before you make a request. Your job is to create a bucket of perception.

Let's look at the effect of context on hiring. Trying to decide whether an executive is right for a job requires you to know contextual factors. On a personality assessment instrument, a retail executive scored high on the aggressiveness scale. The score was far from the norm; you might even call it aberrant. However, evaluating his score relative to all executives within the company showed that his scores were perfectly normal. Many of the executives were aggressive, and if the retail executive didn't express that level of drive, he would be eaten alive by his future colleagues.

Decision makers need context for understanding; they don't think of the content independent of the context. For example, an "argument" can be an interpersonal problem, a judicial viewpoint, or a reason given in a scientific proof. If we see only part of a sentence with the words—the argument—we don't know the context in which to understand the statement.

Misunderstandings occur because people miss the context. If people misunderstand, it can be difficult to persuade them. You can shift the conversation by saying, "Let me put this in the right context...." Putting things in context helps illustrate your argument. This critical step creates meaning and decisions. We should never underestimate the power of positioning things in the right context.

Contrast Your Position

Positioning, according to Jack Trout and Al Ries, is how you differentiate yourself in the mind of your prospect.[4] Changing minds is difficult. By positioning your ideas, you influence perception.

Contrast is the underlining mechanism for positioning your idea, product, service, company, and yourself in the mind of the audience.

CFO Don Lundgren, commenting on the contrast principle, said

> "As a financial guy, you soon realize that people don't care about the actual numbers, just the variance (the contrast). So when you say the revenue for the quarter was $10 million, people immediately ask—how does that compare (contrast) to plan? In fact, often I give an entire pitch to the board with just variance to plan numbers (contrast)."[5]

Using Contrast to Improve Performance

I coached basketball and managed a Little League team for many years. My daughter and son played on some great teams that won championships. At times, part of coaching required placing the right context around the games for the kids. Getting this right was the challenge. Winning included stretching the kids' abilities in a fun and positive environment. Preparing for a particularly difficult basketball team, we challenged the kids by playing against some of the more athletic parents. Having trained against competition that was more difficult, they were ready for this tough team. They won with confidence.

Dealing with a tough management challenge can improve your daily activities. Place the challenge in the right context to motivate your people. These skills aren't just about influencing others; first influence yourself to reach your dreams.

Your Reference Point: Anchors Aweigh

Imagine someone who has a good track record making a mistake. Now imagine someone without that track record making the same mistake. Do you perceive them differently? Most likely. The reference point alters perception. A high price or a low price establishes an anchor from which you will have a difficult time adjusting. Once you set a starting point, it is hard to shift. Even independent thinkers are subject to this effect. Recall that this is one of the perceptual biases in the Laws of Defeat.

The reference point, or anchor, is a special case of the contrast factor. Anchors are prevalent in the marketplace and frame ideas. For example, you compare prices between products. You size up a deal based upon past agreements. The effect happens instantly, without your noticing the anchor that sets up the decision. Again, what is surprising is that we are unaware of the anchor's effect, whether we are professionals, experts, or novices. Just as you can employ the anchoring effect to influence, it's equally important to be prepared for its effect on your own decision making.

Contrast, context, and anchors influence our perception and become even more significant during times of uncertainty.

6. Consistent Expectations

Consistency is a sixth influence factor. The structure of consistency, that people want to act consistent with their views of themselves, is a powerful motivator. Our general belief is that responsible people are consistent, and irresponsible people are inconsistent. Research by Leon Festinger established that consistency is a central motivator for people.[6]

We've all heard the expression that people are only as good as their word. What makes people follow through with what they say they will do? The answer is that we want to be consistent with the expectations we set for ourselves.

Giving people a positive reputation to uphold is an effective influencer. Anwar Sadat, President of Egypt, was known to employ this strategy. According to Henry Kissinger, U.S. Secretary of State, Sadat would acknowledge his bargaining opponent's fair-mindedness and then, during the negotiations, would employ that positive reputation to his advantage.[7]

Expectations Matter

What do you expect of your team? Positive expectations of teams and individuals can produce desired behavior. Sales forces that are treated with high expectations and respect outperform those that are attacked and doubted.

You can improve your influence when you first confirm that the person has the attribute you value—"You're the type of person who…"—and then the person will often live up to the agreed upon expectation. Here are a few examples:

Influencing a key direct report:
"You're the type of person others look to for guidance."
"That tends to be the case."
"Can I count on you to speak up at the meeting today?"
"Okay."

Influencing a vendor:
"You seem to be someone who doesn't say you will do something unless you believe you can follow through. Would that be a fair statement?"
"Yes."
"So when you told us that you will do your best to bring this matter to a successful conclusion before the end of the month, that's something we can look forward to, right?"
"That's right."

Influencing up:
"I see you as someone who will give a fair shake to new ideas."
"Yes."

"I'd like to meet with you next week to discuss some ideas my team has about improving performance. Would that be okay?"

"Sure."

Dissonance

If consistency is so important, what happens when you aren't in accord with your stated or highly held views? It creates dissonance. If you say you are against war but vote to go to war, it creates internal conflict. Leon Festinger makes the case that cognitive dissonance must be resolved: "When attitudes conflict with actions, attitudes, or beliefs, we are uncomfortable and motivated to try to change."[8] You are motivated to resolve the dissonance—to make it okay.

Cognitive dissonance requires people to reduce tension. People will rationalize, deny reality, and minimize the effect. For example, when some people make a bad stock-market decision, it's hard for them to cut their losses because of the dissonance. They want to think they made a good decision and will keep the stock to resolve the dissonance. They might think, "In time, the stock will turn around." We work diligently to be as good as our word or image, and when we aren't, we need to resolve the dissonance in a way that makes it okay with us.

A high-tech manager was hired with the understanding that he would rapidly advance to a senior position in the company. Politics were at play inside the company, but senior leaders told him they knew he should be a vice president and would be promoted soon. However, he was promoted slowly and never reached the vice president level. Eventually, he found a vice president position at another company. The original company didn't keep its word—it was in the throes of cognitive dissonance.

How did the company rationalize not fulfilling its verbal agreement? The leaders weren't lying; the hiring manager sincerely meant to promote him. The story they told themselves was that the business environment had changed and the positions were no longer open as they had been before. This was a rational explanation that reduced the dissonance for the hiring manager.

Using Dissonance

Sales organizations use the foot-in-the-door technique to get small commitments. Over time, they create leverage from dissonance by showing the prospect that by not taking the next step, the prospect is acting inconsistent with the initial commitment.

Sales momentum moves from suspect to prospect, from prospect to customer, from small customer to big customer.

Advantage-Makers employ expectations, consistency, and dissonance to create action.

Now that we are committed to influencing, let's take an exclusive look at the rare skill Advantage-Makers use to influence during uncertainty.

7. Influence During Uncertainty

The most important time to provide leadership influence is during times of uncertainty. The rapid changes we experience create disorder in our midst. Amos Tversky and Daniel Kahneman's landmark work *Judgment under Uncertainty* provides insight into uncharted terrain.[9] These psychologists received the Nobel Prize in economics for their work.

The Prospects of Getting What You Want

Their approach, known as Prospect Theory, illustrates how people make decisions under uncertainty. It informs us of the preferences people tend to make and, in particular, how they see the prospects of a gain or a loss. Our commonsense mental models of how to influence a decision might actually be counterproductive.

In reality, decisions do not follow a straight line. The patterns are not rational, although they are repeatable. People are not logical; they are psychological.

The power of Prospect Theory is that it predicts systematic differences in choices as a function of how options are framed. What do you believe is people's predominant tendency—do they make decisions based upon what they will gain or what they will lose?

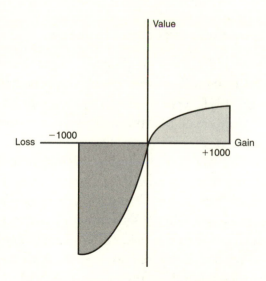

Loss and gain are not perceived equally

Looking at this graph (adapted from Tversky and Kahneman[10]), you can see that loss and gain are not perceived equally. In this example, $1,000 is not just a numerical amount. The same amount of loss is perceived as larger and having more impact than an equal amount of gain. Said another way, a gain of $1,000 is not valued as much as a loss of $1,000.

Most prominent is the effect of frames on you as a decision maker. In the world of frames, $1,000 is not $1,000. This is not logical; however, this is how people make decisions. The prospect of losing is a more powerful motivator than the possibility of gain.

The slope is steeper for losses; losses seem worse to lose than gains seem positive to gain. Loss aversion is more convincing than gain attraction. Consider, for example, how you avoid firing problem makers because you are uncertain if you can replace them in time to get the work completed.

Using Loss Versus Gain to Increase Influence

If your objective is to influence, to get the other party to say yes, it's useful to know how they decide important matters. Entrepreneurs are risk takers and driven by gain—at least, that's the image we have. They create new business and innovative value in products and services. Yet during meetings, I've listened to venture capitalists make investment decisions by framing their argument as "If we don't get into this deal now, someone else will." The prospect of loss drives people's decisions. Framing shapes emotional responses.

Surprisingly, when you frame an issue in terms of what people will gain relative to the risk, decision makers tend to be risk-averse. You tend to be more conservative with your choices when issues are viewed under gain framing. A bird in the hand is worth two in the bush. You might ask yourself if the upside is big enough to make your bet. However, a big opportunity can lead to a riskier decision when the gain is significantly larger. The gain needs to be higher on the S-curve in our graph.

To make a change, the upside gain must be much greater than the downside risk. Proposals fail because the upside is just too small relative to the possible downside. "Why can't they see that they can make these gains?" managers complain. Gains are perceived relative to the cost or the required effort. The risk might not be financial, but operational. Requesting a change in a process might require effort without guaranteeing a dramatic improvement. Losses and problems loom bigger than gains and opportunities. In your proposal, make sure the value is large enough to compensate for risk and effort. Don't assume that the upside is sufficient.

This factor affects negotiations as well. Each side might be offering gains that are perceived as small compared to the sacrifices. Our side has more value; the other side must give up something more substantial in return: "What I have to give up is more important than what I have to gain."

Most of us tend to think gain framing is more motivating. We are goal-oriented and independently go for what we want. This tends to be true when less risk is at stake. Hope for brighter days and aspiration for a better life compel us to action. Ironically, loss framing tends to make decision makers willing to take more risks. When we've been losing, we tend to say to ourselves, "What do I have to lose? I'm already down, so I'll take a chance. It can only go up from here." Hope is a powerful motivator under these conditions.

FedEx CEO Fred Smith reportedly did just this in the early stages of the company when he realized he couldn't meet payroll.[11] What did he do? At a stopover in Las Vegas, he apparently went to the gaming tables and placed his bets. The rest is overnight history. Knowing you might lose something motivates you to take a chance to reduce the loss.

Desire is the impetus for ideas and action. People want what they desire and will take action to avoid losing it. You want to get this car at this price before someone else makes a counteroffer. You'll take action to minimize losing the car.

Organizational Change

During organizational change efforts, followers ask, "Is it worth it, and is the change worth the sacrifice?" Instead of sugarcoating the answer to these questions, the appropriate influence strategy is to state why the change will work—specifically, how things will be worse if you don't make the change, the real sacrifice required, and specific actions for improvement.

A similar communication mistake is repeated when managers don't convey a realistic cost of inaction. An HR manager said he preferred to put a positive spin on things. Although his message was well intended and, at times, appropriate, it was poorly received. Most importantly, it missed the power of loss framing and was out of touch with the real events of the situation.

Scarcity: Rare and Exclusive

Scarcity, the seventh strategic-influence factor, includes the framing of losses and gains. It's the rule of the rare. The scarcity principle is defined as "People assign more value and are attracted to opportunities when they are less available."[12] In other words, rare experiences, materials, resources, information, and efforts are all special. Rare is worth more.

People underutilize the scarcity factor, even though influence agents use it on us from the moment we wake up. In organizations, information is power; the keeper of rare knowledge and know-how is valued more than people who know run-of-the-mill stuff. If you are indispensable—the only one who has the answers or knows how to get them—you have influence power.

Have you ever been to an auction and had auction fever? Auctioneers are masters of scarcity—one-of-a-kind, chance of a lifetime to own, and so on. When people compete for the same resource, scarcity increases the value of the resource. Homes in the San Francisco Bay Area go for astronomical prices, driven in part by scarcity and bidding wars. The real estate agents complain and smile all the way to the bank. If you are always available, you are a commodity. If you are valued and your availability becomes rare, you become invaluable.

Scarcity is inherent in supply-and-demand curves. If supply is greater than demand, prices will be lower. If supply is low and demand is high, scarcity drives up prices. This is a no-brainer. However, the scarcity effect can be manufactured, as in the case when not enough PlayStation 2 systems are available during the holiday rush, which then creates even more demand.

"Take me out to the ball game. Take me out to the crowd. Buy me some peanuts and Crunch 'n Munch." Huh? Cracker Jack has been taken out of the old ball game. There was an uproar at Yankee Stadium, and it wasn't about home runs. "It's un-American," some proclaimed. If you surfed the Internet, you found it was worse than un-American—do so at your own linguistic peril. How can we explain this uproar at Yankee Stadium? Taste tests were performed. Crunch 'n Munch won. However, the tests were never performed with the knowledge that Cracker Jack would no longer be available. What happens when things become less available? They become more valuable, more desired. Bring back Cracker Jack! No less an authoritative newspaper than the *New York Times* had an article titled "Yankees Cut Cracker Jack from Lineup."[13] Yankees fans thought it was sacrilege. We want what we can't have. Lest you think this is only a Yankees-fan foible, it happened with Coke and New

Coke[14] and with many end-of-life products. Take familiar products off the shelves, and we want them back.

Using Scarcity to Create Your Leadership Brand

Niches are, by their nature, selected because of their narrow, specific field. Niche players understand that less is more. Instead of casting a wide net over everyone, businesses select a niche and, when they are right, prosper. Niche players try to corner the market—they specialize. In other words, they want to be the exclusive or rare provider. Victoria's Secret sacrifices all other clothes for its sexy apparel. Have you ever heard of Interstate Department Stores? Most of us haven't. They tried to be all things to all people and went bankrupt. However, there was one exception. They made money on one rare product line: toys. They came out of bankruptcy with a narrow focus on toys. Perhaps you've heard of them: Toys R Us.[15]

How can you as a leader become a rare resource and provide scarce value? The first step is to evaluate the number of people who are ready, willing, and able to match the criteria of the objective. Are you an Advantage-Maker? Are you one of the many or one of the few? Establishing yourself as one of the few increases your professional value. If you are *one of the few* who is ready, willing, and able to contribute to the business success, your stock will go up. On the other hand, if you are just *one of the many* who are ready, willing, and able, you are a managerial commodity. In any business transaction, evaluate the number of entities that are ready, willing, and able. If you have only one option, the other party will control the terms. If you have many options, you will influence the outcome.

This is what branding, in effect, accomplishes. A good brand says you are the only one who provides the product. A solid leadership brand says you are the only one who can take them to the promised land. You own the category. FedEx owns overnight delivery. How much more influential can a delivery business be than owning a place in the customer's mind known as "overnight delivery"?

Effective influence agents appropriately convey that their product or service is scarce. They provide a rare service. You become known as the only one who can solve a certain class of problems.

Rare information takes on a class of its own; it reaches the special place known as *exclusivity*. When you live in the land of exclusivity, you've hit the mother lode.

Listen to news reports—hear an exclusive interview with the Secretary of State.

Watch the Discovery channel—see exclusive pictures of the deepest ocean creatures.

Turn on the music station—hear an exclusive version of the last time the Beatles sang together.

Readership and viewership increase when the headlines contain "new" news. Getting the story first, getting the new news out first, becomes a driving force for the media. Getting it right is a journalistic ethic that sometimes comes in second.

If you have exclusive information, share it, but do so exclusively. To make your exclusive news even more valuable, present it as breaking news. To be an Advantage-Maker, I advise my clients to provide breaking news, not old news. You want to own the new news position, not be tagged as the old news person. We value new, exclusive information. In the world of brands, being the first in the category is comparable to breaking news. Charles Schwab was the first discount broker. He actually made news not as a better broker, but as a new category of broker. Brains pay attention to what is new.

A small, interested group was listening to Cialdini present his latest findings. As he spoke, Bob said he had just received a research article that revealed new influence findings. Everyone instantly and automatically leaned forward to hear the newest and latest in this exclusive opportunity. The scarcity heuristic was operating. Later that day, we discussed his presentation, and Bob pointed out that he would have been a bungler had he not said it was new information. How many times have we bungled the moment of influence by missing its rare qualities that we had the opportunity to preside over?

A National Sales Vice President told me that whenever the company announces the end of a product's life, consumers create a run on the product. It drives sales. The product had been sitting on the shelf, and suddenly people want what will be gone. What advantages would be created if this became part of the sales strategy instead of an afterthought? You can expect that when you make something rare, when you take away an option, it becomes more valuable.

When something becomes precious, we do what is necessary to keep it. Have you ever tried to take away freedom from someone, especially a newly freed person or group? What follows are statements such as "Give me liberty or give me death."[16] The next thing you know, a revolution starts.

Executive Influence

An executive was having trouble getting the CEO to approve his requests. Why hadn't his attempts worked? Together we reviewed his approach. After a few minutes, it became obvious that his attempted influence strategy was always based upon gain framing.

On his next opportunity, he vividly framed the cost of inaction and the losses to the organization. Exclusive, time-sensitive information that was valuable now was contrasted with being worthless later. This was not fabricated. Similar past requests had been bungled, but not this time.

Subsequently, in each new critical request, the executive applied the strategic-influence strategy. Before he consciously used the influence factors, he was turned down about 40% of the time; afterward, his rejection rate was only 20%. His new approach has created a receptive ear in the CEO. In an ironic twist, the CEO thinks the executive is performing better. His credibility is no longer in question; instead, it is simply a matter of influencing.

The rule of the rare includes scarcity, exclusivity, and the prospect of loss framing. You can use the disadvantage of loss to your advantage. Failing to use the scarcity factor will cost you opportunities. The rarest element is time. It is a special factor; it has exclusive rights.

8. When: Time and Timing

Timing, timing, timing—we are creatures of time. Time is our hidden culture. A leader is a woman or man of the times. All the influence skill in the world will fall on deaf ears if your timing is off. Timing is everything. Leaders must always be cognizant of time. Victor Hugo said, "An invasion of armies can be resisted, but not an idea whose time has come."[17] The timeliness of influence is critical. The same joke told with poor timing is not a joke at all.

Timing is a crucial strategic influence factor. What makes the right time? Can you affect timeliness? Let's not waste time, and get right to it.

Time is money. Leveraging time can produce better returns. Employing it for or against a particular argument is a useful practice. It can be a pressure point, as in "Time is running out."

Being at the right place at the right time can seem lucky. It has been said that "Luck is the coincidence of preparedness and opportunity." If you are prepared to use time, opportunities will present themselves in a lucky way.

If you want to create a sense of urgency, shorten the time frame. Deadlines influence action. If you want to influence your people to take action, include a time frame for when to start and when it should be completed. Executives trying to light a fire under people to take action sometimes forget, or miss, the opportunity to say when things need to start and be done. That seems obvious, but in the midst of the action, it can be overlooked. Usually that doesn't last too long.

Conversely, if you want to increase your degrees of freedom in a negotiation, the quickest step is to lengthen your time frame. Compare needing to get something negotiated today versus getting it done next month.

Consider the influence that time played in the ending of the Vietnam War. Negotiating delegations from both the United States and Vietnam booked their hotel accommodations for talks to end the war. The United States booked one month. The North Vietnamese booked several years. They weren't in a rush and knew the United States had political urgency to resolve the conflict now. Upon hearing the Vietnamese hotel time, the U.S. delegation had to rethink its negotiation strategy. The North Vietnamese had strengthened their influence before they even sat down at the negotiating table. Time changes the action and the intensity.

At what point in time does it become a significant problem for you not to have the results you want? This question can set the direction of the conversation. If you have all the time in the world, urgency doesn't exist.

Time is used as a sales accelerator. Most ads are time-bound, and examples are bountiful—this price is good through this weekend only, hurry on down before they're all gone, look the way you want within two weeks. Infomercials convey that operators are waiting for your call, and if you call within the next 15 minutes, you get an additional 30% off. Although many people might justifiably question infomercial products, time used ethically and skillfully can support your objectives.

Time to Ask

Influence comes in all sizes. When my daughter, Samantha, was seven, she used her natural influence talents. One evening, we were getting ready for dinner. I was just about to tell her that the food was on the table when she blurted out "Can I eat down here tonight?" "Uh, okay," I said, and the next thing I knew, I was bringing dinner to her downstairs in the family room. Sometimes the time is ripe, and all you need to do is ask. I made a mental note and always remembered, "Sometimes all you need to do is ask."

At the doctor's office, my physician was making a referral to another specialist. The administrator said the referred doctor didn't have an opening until Christmas (this was in June). I said, "Well, my condition warrants seeing someone sooner, so either she can fit me in or let's find another referral." This would have been a big deal, because it was out of their medical group. The administrator said, "Let me look," and she checked her computer. "Well, how about three weeks from now?" I almost said okay—after all, six months to three weeks was a pretty substantial contrast. We already know how well contrasts work. But then I remembered my daughter's strategy of just asking, and I blurted, "Can you do any better?" The administrator said, "Well, let me see." She came back with, "Next Friday I have one opening that I usually save, just in case." "In case of what?" I thought to myself, half-amused. I now had the week-away appointment. The time was ripe to ask.

Taking too much time can reduce the intensity of desire. "Strike while the iron is hot" is not just an aphorism. If you want to increase the effectiveness of the request, it is important to get your timing right. Research shows that too much time between requests can dampen the effect. Similarly, events that happened long ago are not as troublesome as those we are in the midst of or that we expect to deal with in the near future.

Opportunity Knocks

At what point in time should you make a request? Cialdini contends that answers can be found in the concept of moments of influence, which he labels *Moments of Power,*[18] the title of his upcoming book on the subject. These moments represent windows of opportunity when a request will be most timely and successful. Fortunately, the ability to recognize and use these moments is a learnable skill.

Too many organizational leaders make bad timing decisions with respect to organizational change. They work on issues after they've festered. When you get a scrape, you clean it up right away. If you don't, it can get infected and become a much bigger problem. This tends to be the case more often than not in organizations. A CEO I know said, "The biggest mistake I made was not bringing you in earlier." To his credit, he made the right moves, but it cost him more by waiting. He does not have a monopoly on that category. If your direction is wrong, it takes longer to correct it. Timing and direction are intricately woven together.

The influence rules of thumb are shortcuts. They save us time. We take the advice of experts instead of taking the time to study the issues. It's time well spent if they're right. Presenting the right contrast persuades people to take action now, whereas an ineffective argument without contrast can close a window of opportunity. Appealing to their relevant self-interest can quickly solidify customer relations. Masters of influence track the time horizon for their target audience. They have both a sense of timing and an ability to influence time.

When will the customer be most responsive to your influence? You can create a window of opportunity at these times:

- When you have vividly set the stage that is in the customer's self-interest
- When you give the customer something of value; this initiates reciprocity
- When you make an offer and the customer refuses it, but you have a fallback position
- When the framing contrast makes value stand out
- When things are uncertain and you point to sources similar to the customer
- When being consistent with your word matters
- When you present a credible source that is unbiased
- When the opportunity is new and rare
- When the loss is something the customer wants to avoid

You can use these relationships between the influence strategies and time. Your timing improves when you put the strategic influence factors into play. If you don't recognize the moment as an opportunity, time will pass without moving the action forward.

Timing Your Influence

The target of influence, in effect, is to strategically identify naturally occurring opportunities. Masters of the timing factor know there's no time like the present to create the desired future.

A major technology firm was negotiating with a foreign nation. Progress was made, but then they hit a serious impasse. I was serving as an influence consultant. The senior executive and I analyzed the situation to penetrate to the heart of the negotiation and the negotiators. From the vantage point of strategic influence, the VP made just a few pivotal changes. These included framing the relevant self-interest of the negotiator, establishing an exclusive scarce opportunity, and making a nonarguable contrast with the competition. This advantage-making strategy overcame deal-breaking obstacles and resulted in the purchase of millions of units.

It is the premise of this book that you can capitalize on hidden opportunities, and using the advantage-making strategies can create superior outcomes that matter to you. By applying the hidden opportunities to influence perception, you can shift the odds in your favor. Managers know that when you don't have a lot of time, you need leverage tools to get an edge. Employing the influence factors at the right time provides that edge. A leader without timing won't be influential.

To Influence or Not to Influence

The idea that people are trying to persuade us is not news; that we each hear thousands of appeals yearly is not news. What is unexpected is the level of inadvertent bungling to win the hearts and minds of others. Understanding how perception shifts work is essential. Failures might come from using the wrong strategy. As an Advantage-Maker leader, you are at the epicenter of strategic influence. Using the right influence factors enables you to multiply your efforts to get more from less. Although many things are arguable in companies, Advantage-Makers who know how to persuade usually become the most influential leaders in their organization.

The Advantage-Maker's Advice

Carpe influence, or you will become carp for the sharks.

Tips and Tools for Cultivating Strategic Influence

Evaluate to what degree you are using each of the influence factors with a target audience. Identify a boss, peers, direct reports, customers, prospects, or investors. The pattern of these factors becomes your Web of Influence.

Let's summarize the eight Web of Influence factors:

1.   **Vivid framing**—Relevant self-interest
2.   **Reciprocity**—Building social capital
3.   **Source credibility**—Expertise and authority
4.   **Similarity**—Social validation
5.   **Contrast**—Comparisons and anchor points
6.   **Expect consistency**—You're the type of person who...
7.   **Rare**—Scarcity, exclusivity, loss framing
8.   **Timing**—Expand or contract, create the right time

For example, on a scale of 1 to 10, to what extent are you skillfully employing vivid framing? On the Web of Influence, indicate your score for each factor (1 is in the center, and 10 is on the outside). Connect the dots. The area inside the dots is your influence strength; the area outside the dots is your "opportunity knocking" area. Now you can design influence adjustments for the next opportune time.

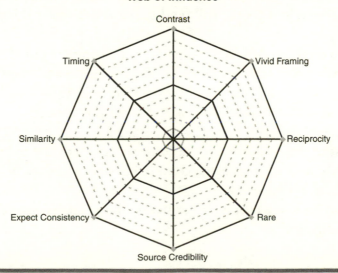

Web of Influence

Recap for Chapters 8 and 9

Chapters 8 and 9 both cover strategic influence. Following is the recap for both chapters:

1. Advantage-Maker leaders are influencers. At critical moments and times of uncertainty, we look for their influence. If you are not influencing, it is difficult to think of yourself—or for anyone else to think of you—as a leader.
2. Influence occurs whenever someone is making a request.
3. Vividly frame relevant self-interest, the gains and pains. Vivid information is more influential than valid information.
4. The reciprocity principle states that when you make a request, you should give something first. Social capital is generated by reciprocity.
5. Bunglers miss the opportunity of influence because they fail to incorporate influence factors into their arguments.
6. Establishing your unbiased authority is paramount for your leadership credibility and influence. Argue against your self-interest, and people will tend to believe the next thing you say.
7. As creatures of social comparison, we compare our views with others who are similar to us to validate and know what is correct—especially in times of uncertainty. Especially during uncertainty, we look to see what is correct.
8. Contrasts—your brain likes them. First contrast, and then make your request. People compare contexts and then draw conclusions. Establish a context for your audience before you make a request.
9. Acting consistent with our word and image is a powerful motivator.

10. Prospect Theory states that avoiding losses has greater impact than gains. Cialdini's scarcity principle states that people assign more value and are attracted to opportunities when they are less available. The rare, exclusive, and new are valued more.

11. Influential leaders know that there's no time like the present to create the future.

Endnotes

1   Robert Fritz, Class, 2000.

2.   Robert Cialdini, in personal conversation, 2004.

3.   John F. Kennedy, inaugural speech, January 20, 1961.

4.   Jack Trout and Al Ries, *Positioning: The Battle for Your Mind* (New York: Warner Books, 1981).

5.   Don Lundgren, CFO, in personal communication, 2006.

6.   Leon Festinger, *The Theory of Cognitive Dissonance* (New York: Harper and Row, 1957).

7.   Robert Cialdini influence review notes, 2003.

8.   Leon Festinger, *The Theory of Cognitive Dissonance* (New York: Harper and Row, 1957).

9.   Amos Tversky and Daniel Kahneman, "Judgment under Uncertainty: Heuristics and Biases," *Science*, 185, 1124–1130, 1974.

10.   Daniel Kahneman and Amos Tversky, "Prospect Theory: An Analysis of Decision under Risk," *Econometrica*, 47 (1979): 263–291.

11.   Seminar story told by Mike Basch, former FedEx executive, 2000.

12.   Robert Cialdini, *Influence: Science and Practice,* 4th ed. (Needham Heights, MA: Allyn & Bacon, 2001).

13. Corey Kilgannon, "Yankees Cut Cracker Jack from Lineup," *New York Times*, May 21 2004, http://aolsvc.news.aol.com/sports/article.adp?id=200908809990009.

14. Cialdini, influence review notes, 2003.

15. Jack Trout and Al Ries, *The 22 Immutable Laws of Marketing* (New York: HarperBusiness, 1993).

16. Patrick Henry, speech delivered 23 March 1775, Richmond, Virginia.

17. Victor Hugo, quotes in Wikipedia, http://en.wikiquote.org/wiki/Victor_Hugo.

18. Robert Cialdini, in personal communication regarding his forthcoming book, 2006.

CHAPTER 10

Being an Advantage-Maker: How to Play in a Different League

*There's only one way to succeed at anything,
and that is to give it everything.*
—*Vince Lombardi*

Not all leaders are Advantage-Makers. Leaders with the penetrating insight and sound judgment of an Advantage-Maker are able to turn situations to their best possible advantage, create superior outcomes in the face of constraints, and guard against the designs of their competitors.

Are you ready to take your advantage-making ability to the next level? Many managers wait too long. And worse, they repeat what they know instead of shifting. This is a surprising and unfortunate conclusion about failing companies and failing executives. In times of disruption, they rely upon the same strategy they used to succeed in the past.

Advantage-Makers are originators. Their impulse is original. To originate requires a shift. In a practical sense, new products and services aren't introduced every day, but a capacity for fresh thinking exists every day.

Advantage-making leaders do things differently. They can be dangerous to conventional approaches—things will change.

Advantage-making is not as much creativity as it is shifting.

Will you engage in strategic shifts when you encounter challenges? In essence, the Code of the Advantage-Maker is based upon shifts—more specifically, shifting time, interactions, perceptions, and structures. Therefore, at your core, have you deliberately cultivated the capacity to shift?

This is not a once-you-read-it-now-you're-done type of talent. Getting to the eighth-floor Advantage Point is essential, but not easy. You won't get there by continuing to do more of the same old, same old. If you want to play in this different league, you must practice the craft of advantage-making.

Advantage-Making Is a Craft

Professional actors think of acting as a *craft*. Excelling in their craft requires learning specific distinctions to get into character. Musicians work on scales to keep their skills honed. Similarly, advantage-making is a craft that improves with practice.

As an Advantage-Maker, detecting hidden opportunities are the "scales" you practice. You want to see opportunities where others see only problems, to influence outcomes where others are stuck, and to create solutions where others are challenged.

It is said that decisions are made by those who show up. In a comparable way, advantages are made by your showing up and seizing the opportunity. Your curiosity maintains the momentum.

To excel at the craft of advantage-making and see what others don't see, always apply the four Advantage Point levers—practice adaptive stretching, be a game-changer, move or lose, and apply strategic influence.

Use these ideas on an as-needed basis, and they will support your efforts. However, your craft is not a part-time job; the quality of your advantage-making is at stake.

Do the Most with the Hand Dealt to You

While working with George Prince, CEO of Synectics, we engaged in a research project to understand how to manage innovation with others. In Chapter 5, "Adaptive

Stretching: It's Not the Best Who Wins—It's Who's the Most Adaptive," I cited George's ability to innovate and create. One of the profound things we discovered was an ongoing private question that innovators employ. In George's case, his personal question was, "Am I making this 'situation' what it could be?"

This question orients and reveals an internal drive—an ambitious curiosity. George's strong intent and his way of operating had two tendencies: He would shift to different vantage points to view the issues, and he would imagine what those situations could be.

In other words, he was generating a world of possibility. George's ongoing sensibility was to make these possibilities practical, workable realities. Increasing the chances of spotting an opportunity begins with exercising the craft.

Contrast George's approach with a CEO who made a lot of money on a single business proposition that he implemented. It worked—until the market changed and he couldn't change with it. A difference exists between those who have an advantage-making spirit and those who achieve a one-time win. The CEO stopped looking for vantage points; his personal question was something such as, "Is this working?" Similar to a thermostat, he wasn't thinking or considering anything that could be done.

If you would like to walk in the shoes of a great innovator and Advantage-Maker, you might want to try on George's question: "Am I making this 'situation' what it could be?"

The implication behind the words is that you ought to "get going" on considering the possibilities. George would *constantly* look at situations, problems, and constraints from different vantage points. Experiment with this and see how it works for you.

Personal-orienting questions are powerful. They identify the first perceptual filter. For example, if your orienting question is "How will they use this against me?", it narrows your craft of advantage-making and makes it more difficult for you.

Advantage-making is a full-time position. By shifting to any of the Advantage Points, you can transform the current situation into an unexpected bonus. Some managers wait to use the skill; more proficient Advantage-Makers apply the advantage-making toolkit to the challenge in front of them. Similar to George, they get the most out of the hand dealt them. Doing so requires you to go beyond your zone of familiarity.

Show the Fly the Way Out of the Bottle

Every now and then, a proverbial fly becomes stuck in an open bottle. In vain, the fly repeatedly bangs its head against the sides of the bottle. The fly doesn't see the easy way to escape—finding the opening at the top of the bottle and flying free. Your job as an Advantage-Maker is to "show the fly the way out of the bottle," as the philosopher Wittgenstein would say.[1] We can learn a lot of what not to do by observing the stuck fly.

To create an advantage, you must see a dimension that others aren't looking at, or use a dimension that others aren't using. Adding a dimension in your thinking can be as simple and direct as the following example.

A truck was stuck, pinned under an overpass. It held up traffic for hours. The police, the fire department, and the city's civil engineers were perplexed and bewildered as to how to get the truck out without destroying the overpass, and doing it rapidly. Cars were backing up; reports on the radio were incessant. Careers were being challenged. Nothing seemed to be working until a young girl watching the situation from the service road said, "Why don't they let the air out of the tires?" It worked. With the air out of the tires, the truck lowered and could slowly back up. The trouble was over.

Just as the truck was stuck under the overpass, the professional helpers were stuck in their frame. They couldn't see anything until a wiser, more "mature" set of eyes looked at the problem.

Lucky guess? Or was it that the little girl could see what others couldn't see? She wasn't tainted and narrowed in her field of vision. Her thoughts hadn't solidified to the predictable. She wasn't old enough to have developed sophisticated abstract-thinking skills. At the time, she wasn't ruled by the need for consistency or the usual conventional solutions. Instead of the predictable ideas, she saw what was obvious—that is, she saw what there was to see. This resulted in her actually thinking about it in an original way, a way no one else had looked at it, and she came up with a solution no one else had considered. She was a thought leader and an Advantage-Maker.

Although our young friend clearly was an Advantage-Maker in this setting, we can't yet bestow upon her the crown of advantage-making leader. This would require an ongoing orientation, commitment, and consistency to advantage-making. But she has a great start.

You can be an Advantage-Maker in every role you play, ranging from world shakers to the everyday mom and dad. Are you seizing the opportunity? Chances abound to practice the craft and gain an edge in all areas of your life.

Continuously applying the strategic-shifting tools transforms your leadership into an advantage-making craft. Imagine increasing your odds to be able to do what others say can't be done. That's the pleasure of an Advantage-Maker.

For Jim Bailey, CEO of Accenia, advantage-making is a practical, everyday concern. He described his advantage-making approach as follows:

"Finding ways to increase your hit rate, the success rate. There will always be problems and there will always be choice. We need to leverage our strength to win. For instance, let's consider sales with ten different prospects. Out of ten prospects, two will not buy, two will always buy, and there are the big six in the middle. Developing strategies to have a better win rate with those six is key."[2]

Advantage-making leaders promote transformation; they continuously look for how they can leverage their resources, similar to David against Goliath—using something small to defeat something big. They go beyond the ordinary; with judgment informed by the unanticipated, they achieve the unexpected.

As an Advantage-Maker, you shift between strategic moves and tactical angles, between confronting objective reality and influencing perceptions to create reality, between employing big forces at play and small relevant distinctions, between the expected and the unexpected, and between using the rules and creating new rules that make a difference.

Lyndall Frye, Vice President of Quality, described an Advantage-Maker as a person who "creates the catalyst to move across the gap or create the gap behind you against your competitor. It can actually create the chasm by setting the new standard, a new benchmark, or with new products and services."[3]

Advantage-Makers set up the conditions for leverage, getting the most out of the expected and pursuing the unexpected; similar to early-morning fishermen, they take to the seas *every day*, doing their part, casting the nets, and working until they get their catch. Their net is designed to get the timing right, leverage interactions, influence perceptions, and employ the structural forces at play.

When I asked Bob Cialdini, author of *Influence*, to describe his advantage-making approach, he said: "I try to take things beyond the settings I find them in. I look for the salient feature in situations and consider how this plays in the interactions I deal with on a regular basis."[4] This is simple and profound. You can experiment with this approach as part of your advantage-making craft.

To find the keys, we must look closely at reality. Marv Tseu, Chairman of Plantronics, says "The big key for creating leverage is to see reality clearly. Without that, your judgment becomes suspect."[5] You need to get out of the mental rut; practicing the Advantage Points improves your maneuverability. They help you out of the entrenched angle that limits your perspective.

Ideas sometimes get fused that reduce our ability to see solutions. Our young let-the-air-out-of-the-truck-tires Advantage-Maker didn't get stuck and suggested the obvious. The willingness of leaders to challenge their own views can open their eyes to see the obvious for the first time. And, more importantly, solutions hidden in plain sight.

In a Different League

Advantage-Makers are in a different league. Growing the advantage-making capacity distinguishes advantage-making leaders from traditional leaders. Your advantage-making capacity can grow, and for organizations, the contribution grows straight to the bottom line.

Steve Little, Vice President of Sales, describes the thinking that occurs in this different league:

"You have to practice seeing all the interactions on a playing board, not a two-dimensional, flat board, but a three-dimensional view that enables you to look around the board. A two-dimensional view doesn't let you see the relative position; you can become numb, insensitive, fooled into thinking you know what is going on; you need a field of vision to see all the players, the key gaps, the key openings so you can mobilize and get in position to be in front. And this must be an active process."[6]

The Nerve to Decide

In my interviews with Advantage-Makers, I asked if they had ever missed an opportunity. Although each immediately said yes—partly amused and mostly disappointed with themselves—all recognized opportunities that didn't work out. Sometime along the way, they had all failed. However, what was interesting was the reason they didn't take advantage of some opportunities, and why they had backed out of situations that eventually became successful. As with all of us, they were too bogged down in their own point of view.

If you are to be an Advantage-Maker, you must make forward-moving decisions.

One error was second-guessing themselves. Fear took its toll. Sometimes they were too involved in one thing to change horses, or so they told themselves at the time. In a few instances, an authority or expert they relied upon turned out to be wrong. A CEO said that at an earlier point in her career, she had listened to the "genius" on the staff who had said something couldn't work, and she "took it as gospel." Tens of millions of dollars later, the success of a competitor with that so-called "it couldn't work" business proved to be an expensive lesson.

An acquaintance of mine is a member of the National Science Association and a professional code breaker. He specializes in keeping people locked out of systems. We were discussing the thought process involved in his work during lunch at a restaurant,

Wittgenstein's (named after the brilliant philosopher), in San Francisco. While we were eating, he pointed out what you weren't supposed to notice, by design, in the restaurant. The restaurant had a cozy ambience, but if you looked closely (meaning with code-breaker eyes), the ceilings were unusually high, with very long lighting fixtures that hung from the 30-foot ceilings, giving the place a cozier, smaller feel than the building actually had. You weren't supposed to look at the high ceilings, and it worked. The code breaker's talent enabled him to see what the distractions were designed to keep you from seeing.

What is grabbing your attention and keeping you from creating advantages?

When you shift to notice the everyday distractions that lock you in, preventing you from seeing opportunity, you activate your advantage-making talents.

The Advantage of Hopelessness

If you consistently mishandle difficulty and cannot find hidden opportunity, it's useful to recognize the hopelessness of your approach. When understood for what it actually is, hopelessness is simply a directional signal. It tells you that what you are doing is not working and that you should change directions. Remember, you are not hopeless—only the strategy or objective is hopeless. Don't deny, distort, or delay. Hopelessness is a useful advantage-making tactic in your Advantage Point toolkit. Continuing to do more of the same will take you out of the game. I want you to stay in the game. In other words, when you do something different, there is hope.

When you are playing against other Advantage-Makers, the game heats up. You want to select your executive team from the people who are "in a different league." Their advantage-making abilities can build the capacity to jump from advantage to advantage.

Your advantage-making is the "wind beneath the wings" of great possibility.[7] Creating the future will be the time of your life.

Keep Your Eye on the Ball, and Adjust Your Bat to Where the Ball Is

Little League baseball games are known for high scores. In one game, my daughter's team (a combined boys and girls team) lost by a score of 17–4. I was the manager of the team, and at the next practice, we focused on hitting. During my daughter's turn at bat, she could hardly hit anything, yet we knew she was a terrific athlete. One of the coaches kept calling out the fundamental refrain "Keep your eye on the ball."

I walked up to her and whispered in her ear, "Samantha—keep your eye on the ball."

She immediately said, "I am!" That surprised me, yet I believed her. How could she be keeping her eye on the ball, yet missing it by a mile? I stepped back and reflected about her understanding of our message—"Keep your eye on the ball."

The answer became obvious. I went to the pitcher's mound and, with the ball in hand, said, "If the ball is pitched high, where do you swing your bat?"

"Up high," she said.

"If the ball is low, where do you swing the bat?"

"Down low."

"And if the ball is right down the middle, where do you swing the bat?"

"In the middle."

"Okay, so when we say 'Keep your eye on the ball,' what we really mean is to keep your eye on the ball and adjust your bat to where the ball is."

I pitched the ball, and she whacked it over the shortstop's head. Another pitch, and one bounce to the wall. Every kid learned this: Keep your eye on the ball, and adjust your bat to where the ball is.

When we faced that team again, their boys yelled to move in when the girl (my daughter) came up to bat. Let's just say we beat that team 22–12. After the game, their manager came up to me and asked what I did to these kids. A trade secret, I told him.

Communicate your advantage-making idea, or it might never materialize.

But it isn't a trade secret any longer. When you confront constraints, apply the advantage-making approach and strategically shift to the Advantage Points (adapt and stretch, change the game, move or lose, and strategic influence).

To shift the odds in your favor:

Keep your eye on the ball, and adjust your bat to where the ball is.

The Advantage-Maker's Advice

Constraints can be daunting, placing you against the odds.
Only unexpected strategies can beat the odds.

One person's nuance is another's spotlight.
How well do you intentionally shift your perceptions?

Shift the odds by purposely changing dimensions.
Your spirit will spot it.

Tips and Tools for Advantage-Making

1. **Position at the right vantage point (Starbucks, Charles Schwab Brokerage).** From their vantage point, they changed industries, targeting and identifying the driving forces. Their question is "What really matters to the customer?"

2. **Choose a specific opportunity and an expected future (electronics industry).** The electron was discovered but didn't have any use. Progress is generated from basic science. The questions are "If I approach it from that vantage point, what would it take?" and "What rules can we use to our advantage?"

3. **Clarify the significance of the opportunity (Home Depot).** The executives who started Home Depot could see the significance of the opportunity they had spotted. The Advantage-Maker's questions are "What can this do for our customer?" and "What is the mutual potential here?"

4. **Establish a professional creator's orientation (objectivity) (Microsoft, GE).** They know where they're going and have a good grasp on reality—staying in the game, persisting in the face of adversity. The Advantage-Maker asks, "What are we after, and where are we now?" Don't take yourself out of the game.

5. **Originality, ingenuity, and transformation (Apple Computers, Southwest Airlines).** Look for invention, connection-making, and the opportunity to change the rules of the game. Ask the cool questions; be the blue-sky thinker: "What would be cool? What connections exist between what I am working on and nature? What constraints can we reduce?"

6. **Apply the appropriate effort simply, efficiently, and directly (Dell Computers).** Use an economy-of-means approach. Dell had a huge cost advantage in direct-mail sales. Ask what Dell did: "How can we do this more simply? How can we reduce the hindrances that everyone is taking for granted? Where is the system broken and we don't realize it?"

7. **Attentive to wide-ranging feedback (Wells Fargo ATMs).** Listen to customers: Ask "What do the customers do, and how can we make their tasks simpler? What is the job the customer is trying to do, and how can we make it better for them? What are customers asking for?"

8. **Customize to the requirements of the end user (Nordstrom).** Go the extra mile. Ask "What would be special that customers don't dare to ask for, but want? How can we change their expectations to a higher level?"

Chapter Recap

1. Advantage-making is the consistent ability to create superior outcomes by leveraging assets in the face of constraints; it's shifting the odds in your favor.
2. Advantage-Makers are in a different league. They are inquisitive and acquisitive in developing their advantage-making capacity. They make more connections, experiment more, learn more, fail more, and rebound quicker.
3. Leaders become Advantage-Makers through the rigorous application of the four Advantage Points (Adapt and Stretch, Change the Game, Move or Lose, Strategic Influence).
4. Do the most with the hand you were dealt. Ask "Am I making this situation what it could be?"
5. Spotting advantages is the key. Nuance is highlighted in the beginning. Don't dismiss the little clues, the anomalies.
6. Be wary of deferring to the genius. They see what they see, and you see what you see. Cultivate the nerve to decide. Leverage the constraints.
7. One added dimension is that, in the final analysis, the human spirit can shift the odds in your favor when you are up against all odds.

Endnotes

1. Ludwig Wittgenstein, *Tractatus Logico-Philosophicus* (New York: Routledge Classics, 2001, original 1921).
2. Jim Bailey, CEO, in Advantage-Maker interview research, 2004.

3. Lyndall Frye, Vice President of Quality, in Advantage-Maker interview research, 2003.

4. Robert Cialdini, Ph.D., author of *Influence*, in Advantage-Maker interview research, 2005.

5. Marv Tseu, Chairman of the Board for Plantronics, in Advantage-Maker interview research, 2004.

6. Steve Little, Vice President of Sales, in Advantage-Maker interview research, 2004.

7. Composers Larry Henley, Jeffrey Silbar, "Wind Beneath My Wings," 1982.

The Advantage-Maker Website

Visit my website, www.advantagemaker.com:

- For more information, further materials or to raise questions
- To find out about advantage-making services or my availability for speeches
- To submit your own examples of advantage-making or of people you believe are outstanding Advantage-Makers
- The annual Advantage-Maker of the Year will also be announced on the website.
- Please submit candidate's names and, if available, contact information for Advantage-Maker of the Year as well.

Index

T

THE SELF-DESTRUCTIVE HABITS
OF GOOD COMPANIES
...And How to Break Them

By Jagdish N. Sheth

Why do so many good companies go bad? In this book, the authors describe the companies that were once thought of as great companies—A&P, Sears, Xerox, Kodak, GM, Corning, Atari, Wang—and how they ended up self-destructing. Readers of *The Self-Destructive Habits of Good Companies....And How to Break Them* can avoid the mistakes of these companies and have a chance to go into turnaround—and perhaps go on to greater heights and greater profits. This book identifies seven dangerous habits even well-run companies fall victim to: denial, complacency, overdependence on traditional competencies, competitive myopia, an obsession with volume, rising culture conflict and turf wars, and arrogance. It then helps readers diagnose their own companies. Most important, they'll find specific, detailed techniques for "curing," or better yet, preventing, every one of these self-destructive habits.

ISBN 9780131791138 ■ © 2007 ■ 304 pp. ■ $24.99 USA ■ $29.99 CAN

WHAT'S YOUR STORY?
Storytelling to Move Markets, Audiences, People, and Brands

By Ryan Mathews and Watts Wacker

Storytelling is a universal human activity. It is universal in that every society, at every stage of history, has told stories. It is human because stories are how people tell each other who they are; where they came from; how they are different from their neighbors; what they worship; and what they believe. Stories capture people's memory of their past and their hopes for the future. Businesses tell stories all the time, but without the discipline of the trained storyteller. Storytelling has a wide variety of business applications, many of which go all but ignored today. In a commercial world where consumers are bombarded by a multitude of often conflicting stories, and where they are no longer satisfied with being members of a passive audience, it is more critical than ever that formal storytelling be adopted as a business tool. Not only do today's storytellers need to know how to craft a story, they now carry the added burden of crafting a context for that story, providing a back story that makes their main story credible. *What's Your Story?* offers business readers a comprehensive storytelling tool chest and practical help in executing a modern storytelling strategy in their companies.

ISBN 9780132277426 ■ © 2008 ■ 240 pp. ■ $24.99 USA ■ $29.99 CAN